Memories & Spice

From South Beach to Southern Spain, A Truly Different Cookbook!

by
Fred Valdes MD

Cork Hill Press
Indianapolis

CORK HILL PRESS™

Cork Hill Press
7520 East 88th Place, Suite 101
Indianapolis, Indiana 46256-1253
1-866-688-BOOK
www.corkhillpress.com

Trade Paperback Edition: 1-59408-193-X

Printed in the United States of America

1 3 5 7 9 10 8 6 4 2

A fun and irreverent tale about the romantic and travel adventures (laced with some cool recipes) of a South Beach (Miami, Fl) surfer who decided to go to medical school in Southern Spain.

This is a project that started back in 1985 based on my wish to write a cookbook that featured not only the recipes, but also the circumstances when those recipes were used. The recipes are unique, and in some cases may be familiar to the reader. I have added a "twist" here and there. The stories...they are all true. Of course the names, time sequences and places have been altered to protect the not so innocent!

You must understand now, I don't want you to get lost in the stories! I want you to try the recipes. There is no particular style of cuisine in this book; however there is a strong Cuban-South Florida influence. If you are reading this book in Nebraska, it may be difficult to find some of the ingredients. That's ok, I have provided some alternatives.

I might also point out that this is not a "diet" book nor is it politically correct. Most events occurred circa 1974-1980 (I think).

I really hope you enjoy this book as much as I did, don't look for 100% accuracy in the recipes and have fun!

SOMEWHAT OF AN INDEX

1) - SOUTH BEACH DOLPHIN   2

2) - CLAM CHOWDER MIAMI   4

3) – AWSOME NEWSOME'S ARROZ CON POLLO   6
(Newsome's Chicken and Rice)

4) - MADUROS! (Sweet Plantains)   8

5) - LA PAELLA DE NILDA (Nilda's Paella)   9

6) - ORANGE BOWL PINCHITOS   12

7) - SHRIMP AND CRAB CRIOLLO   13

8) - CHICKEN A-1-A   15

9) - RAINY DAY CHICKEN SOUP (The Blues Killer)   16

10) - COOL CAULIFLOWER MACARENA   18

11) - CARNE CON PAPAS UFO'S (UFO's Beef Stew)   19

12) - HAVANA BEANS DREAMING   22

13) - BASIL TOMATOES   23

14) - MANGO TANGO ⤳ 24

15) - SHRIMP AND CHICKEN SUNSET ⤳ 26

16) - SEMI-HINDU CHICKEN ⤳ 28

17) - OSSO BUCCO A LA "SAUESERA" ⤳ 33

18) – LEO'S PIG ⤳ 34

19) – ALICIA'S LINGUINI ⤳ 36

20) – SURVIVAL TORTILLA (Survival omelet) ⤳ 40

21) – MACHO CHILI ⤳ 43

22) - ROPA VIEJA (Cuban Shredded Beef) ⤳ 46

23) - DUPREE'S SEAFOOF AND CHICKEN ⤳ 48

24) - DECISION CHICKEN ⤳ 52

25) - GREAT BALLS OF FIRE! ⤳ 53

26) - DELIA'S BOLICHE ROAST ⤳ 54

27) – CHRISTMAS SALMON INSTEAD ᔇ *56*

28) – PINO'S LAMB CHOPS ᔇ *57*

SPICES, SPICES, SPICES ᔇ *63*

BEER ZONE ᔇ *65*

WINE ZONE ᔇ *65*

A LITTLE MORE SPICE ᔇ *68*

Acknowledgements

There are many who in so many ways contributed to make this book possible. I would like to mention some of them. Janet has supported me in every crazy project I have ever come up with. I love her. Vanessa and Monique brought me drinks and kept me company during those late nights like the good night owls they are. All those at City College, Ft. Lauderdale, from the computer people who listened to all my technically intricate questions like "do I also have to turn the screen on?" to Mr. CM Fike II, president of City College who wished that I make my first million with the book (May God hear you CM). Jim Howard who told me "that dog will hunt" and kept my "southernism" flowing, Mr. B "can do", Barbara K. for her encouragement, Jeff (God bless Texas!), Brenda, Adrianne (May some of her organizational skill rub on me) and so many other technical advisors I could not possibly mention here.

Ed Ponce typed the first rough manuscript, Angelo Fuster provided spiritual guidance from Atlanta. See "Awesome Nancy's Chicken and Rice". Angelo and Ed are detailed in that recipe back in Pine Lake, Ga. What a great summer that was! The three of us go back to…well, middle earth even though we still look just past thirty.

My good friend Scarlet who read the first pages and urged me to finish this project.

My English teacher at Miami High, Mr. English (his real name). Mary Janet-Taylor, editor of "The Good Times" at Florida International University who taught me what "indent" meant. The Spades from Jacksonville, our good friends that have shared many cooking experiences with me.

My students at City College who challenge me all the time. My mother who always told me I could do anything I wanted if I engaged my brain. My father who taught me toughness by example.

Lastly, I'd like to mention four people who have inspired me to achieve more. Rush Limbaugh (mega dittos), William F. Buckley (whom I met during a college lecture). Tom Clancy and Clive Cussler. Keep on writing! And to all those who are part of the stories in the book, where ever you are, thank you for crossing my path. It was my gain.

The first recipe is named after South Beach which seems fitting since there is where it all started back in the times when the Beach Boys were younger and Jimmy Buffet had not written "A Pirate Looks at Forty" yet. South Beach is located at the Southern most end of Ocean Drive in Miami Beach. This was the local surfing spot where on any given Saturday one could smell the coconut suntan oil all the way from the McArthur causeway. The local high school players often played sand football here. (Of course, Miami High players were the best). One could get a delicious large slice of pizza and a soft drink for less than two dollars at a small stand called Joe's (no, this was not in the 40's or 50's, this was in the 70's). Joe's was located at the very tip of South Beach on the parking lot of the old dog race track. This was before South Beach became the famous "Art Deco District" and beer started to cost $9.00 dollars a bottle. Joe, the owner of Joe's (no kidding!) would also provide surfing information over the phone which he answered simply with "SOUTH". After leaving the US Army in 1971, I started to entertain thoughts of medical school. I had trained as a medic / lab-technician, MOS 92-B-20 for those in the military and this prompted an interest. While attending Florida International University and trying to get accepted into different medical schools without success, Spain became an option as I was told many Americans were going to medical schools overseas. Many of my dreams and songs were inspired under the breeze and surf sounds of South Beach. Perhaps this book can help re-kindle or find some new dreams for you.

So, let's get started.

It was a typical June Miami morning when I woke up with the sun's heat upon my face. Thinking of Fred Neil's song called "Saturday's Child"; I looked outside my window to welcome a perfect cloudless blue sky, and the coconut trees being swayed by a decent breeze. I have always liked the breeze, it helps you walk through the rough times when it's at your back and it helps build your endurance when you walk against it. Breeze also meant there might be some decent waves at South Beach and after washing down a hunk of buttered Cuban toast with orange juice and café con leche (Cuban coffee and milk) I headed out with my surfboard and my old guitar. All I had in mind that day were perhaps a few decent waves and playing some tunes. Making sure there was enough gas in the tank, I crossed over the McArthur causeway heading for South Beach. I walked down the pier and was watching a seagull dip for food when a tall blonde caught my eye (actually both of my eyes, why do we say "my eye" when we use both?). I did not recall seeing her before and based on her still pale skin, assumed she was new to the beach. One can burn real bad on a day like that without protection, so, in the spirit of community service, (one of my finest qualities) I approached her and introducing myself offered to rub some home made sun tan oil produced by a friend of mine in which he uses some aloe plant sap and other rare stuff that seems to work pretty good. Since it's hard to reach your own back I volunteered to rub the stuff on her back myself and a conversation ensued. Her name was Paula, native of Omaha, Nebraska, corn-fed all the way! Things went well. She confessed this was the first time she had seen an ocean, imagine that? After a couple of days of fun in the sun, surfing lessons and playing some of my original songs for her, Paula invited me to meet her aunt who had moved to Miami years back. I agreed and since I had told Paula about my cooking skills, she *suggested I show her aunt what I could do. Yep, here comes the first recipe, I know you were beginning to wonder if this was really a cookbook ha?*

1-SOUTH BEACH DOLPHIN

I asked a friend of mine whose father owns a commercial fishing boat to get me some fresh Dolphin. For those of you in Rio Linda or Omaha, this is NOT Flipper ok, this is a fish, also called Mahi Mahi in some places. That Saturday night I arrived at her aunt's house with all the ingredients and some flowers, a bottle of Marques Del Riscal Blanc was placed in the freezer. Let's cook man!

- Two lbs of fresh dolphin filet

- One large onion sliced thin

- 3 large (yes large) cloves of garlic chopped small

- One cup of dry sherry or dry white wine. (If you can't drink it, don't use it)

- 1/2 cup of fresh parsley diced (don't forget to wash it)

- 1 tsp salt

- 1 tsp pepper

- Juice of one lime

- 1/4 cup olive oil (Goya, Carbonell, Sensat) Get Spanish olive oil, not that Italian bland stuff.

- 10 or more manzanila olives, pimento stuffed work great.

Here is what you do:
Marinate the fish in the wine, garlic and limejuice and olives for a couple of hours (more if you can), do it in the refrigerator if more than two hours, covered of course. In a medium or large pan, sauté the onions in the olive oil until they are clear, about 2 minutes. Make room in the middle of the pan and add the fish, salt and pepper and parsley, medium heat, cook for about 7 minutes depending on how thick the fillets are, turn over carefully with a spatula and cook until fillets are flaky and tender. White rice, steamed baby carrots and green beans, make sure you finish the wine ok.

Diner went fine; Paula's aunt was impressed and told me I'd be a popular guy in Nebraska (they don't surf there do they?). After some Cuban coffee we took a walk on the beach near the so called Jetties, a man made boulder formation that forms the entrance on the ocean to Biscayne Bay, the entrance is called Government Cut and it IS a great place to sit and howl at the moon or tell sea stories by the light of the moon which was full and orange color, in the distance we could see the lights of a freighter or a cruise ship becoming brighter in the horizon. We held hands, I mentioned about my possible plans to go to medical school in Spain that coming fall and somehow at that point we knew that the chances of seeing each other again were as remote as the orange moon or a snowfall in Miami. When she got back to Nebraska I received a perfumed letter with a box of frozen Omaha steaks, I sent her a picture of the beach and a box of oranges. Did I consider a trip to Nebraska? Maybe for a moment, but I did not go, I am a tropical guy, I need to hear Jimmy Buffet, the sound of the surf, palm trees swaying in the summer breeze! Little did I know that would all change very soon...

Summer went and I embarked in a new phase of my life, medical school in Spain! I won't go into details of the arrival; it still seems like a blur even after all these years. After surviving the first semester and for reasons of keeping my sanity, I came back to the states during the Christmas break. After a few days of being home, some friends invited me to go "clamming" at Sebastian Inlet and fixed me up with a date. If you are from Montana, clamming is digging for clams in ice-cold murky water up too your waist! Sebastian Inlet is near the town of Jupiter in South-central Florida. You find the clams, mostly with your toes and dig them up with a rake and into a basket, this sounds insane, but there was actually a degree of competition and satisfaction in finding the most clams. We managed to get a good amount of clams and I suggested clam chowder would be the perfect meal for a cold night back at the campsite. We were three couples, two were married and my date was the sister of one of the wives who was always trying to find me a "match". Kathy actually turned out to be not only attractive but mentally interesting, a rare combination. At sunset, we headed back to the camping area, I was frozen! 62 degrees is cold for this guy ok, plus we were totally wet and muddy! After a warm shower (no, not together unfortunately) I got into some jeans and a University of Miami sweatshirt (GO CANES!!), we all drank some Cuban coffee and Cardenal Mendoza brandy, life was back. Everyone was hungry though, so I gathered the ingredients and went to work on...

2-CLAM CHOWDER MIAMI

- One pound or more of clams. We used the ones we had dug up which meant they had to be rinsed and brushed very well. If you are not near an inlet and do not want to go "clamming", cans or frozen clams can fulfill the role, use the juice as well.

- Two bottles of clam juice.

- One quart of half and half. I told you this is not a diet book.

- One large onion, diced.

- 1/2 pound of cooked bacon

- 2 sticks of medium salted real butter don't use that "I can't believe it's not butter" stuff ok.

- Two 8 oz. Cans of sweet corn, Del Monte's fresh harvest are great.

- 3 large potatoes, Idaho's ok. Cubes in half inch pieces.

- 8 oz. Of dry sherry, white of course.

In a large heavy pot, melt the butter over medium heat, throw potatoes, onion and sauté until potatoes are fairly cooked but not mush! Add the rest of the ingredients, stir slowly, cover the pot and cook for 45 minutes. If you use fresh clams, the bigger they are, the tougher the chew, I like the medium size ones. If you use the big fresh clams, they should be chopped into smaller pieces. The finished product should have a creamy texture. Salt and pepper should be added to taste. Some fresh Cuban bread will be a tremendous asset to this dish.

We finally started to warm up and ate double portions of the soup with a few glasses of Gato Negro sauvignon Blanc, a great wine from Chile. Afterwards we had Cuban coffee followed by a bottle of Cardenal Mendoza brandy I had brought from Spain. The Chili Florida night unfolded above us with a burst of diamonds on black velvet, Kathy was close to me, for heat conservation of course, across the distant horizon, a shooting start traced its path, no more stories needed to be told that night, events were recorded on the sand and blown into eternity by the morning wind...

SO! How did you like them clams? They say that there is no scientific documentation on the sexual enhancement properties of oysters and clams, yet, that night at Sebastian Inlet may prove all those theories wrong.

Now it's time to go to a more complicated dish, which only Cubans can make it justice. Arroz con Pollo! One my favorite dishes, Yellow Rice and Chicken for those in Rio Linda, California or Omaha, Nebraska. Cubans cook this dish in a very special way. There are a few variations depending of where you grew up in Cuba or even if you grew up in Miami. I will show you my version ok. I have cooked this dish many times, but one those times, stands out in my memory hard drive. It was during the summer of 76 in Atlanta, Ga. I was home from my second year of Medical school and after visiting my parents and friends in Miami; I went to reunite with my brothers Ed and Angelo who at the time lived in Atlanta. We go back... well, almost back to middle earth and believe me, it would take a thick book to tell all of our stories together, so, I am going to relate this one specific night in the Atlanta suburb called Pine Lake where I asked a date with a real cute nurse from the hospital where I was working that summer. Her name? Well, you probably guessed it, Nancy Newsome. I decided to call this dish:

3-AWSOME NEWSOME'S CHICKEN AND RICE

Here is what you need to get, yeah, chicken, you guessed that one already.

- 4 pounds of chicken in pieces, you know, breasts, legs, thighs and some of those mystery pieces you find at KFC

- 2 pounds of Valencia rice, this is the short grain rice, it will not work with the regular long grain rice.

- One 8 oz jar of sweet red roasted peppers, or red roasted sweet peppers. I like Goya fancy brand, however, if you want to get some of the Italian stuff, that's ok, I'll forgive you.

- One small can of tomato sauce, (Goya, Diana, DelMonte)

- 6 oz of DRY sherry

- Two cans of beer (one is for you to drink while you cook)

- 4 large garlic cloves minced

- 1/2 cup of Spanish olive oil (Sensat, Goya, Carbonell are great brands)

- One small box of Saffron (about 20 hairs, see spice page)

- 3 cubes of chicken bullion (Knorr is good)

- One large diced onion

- One spoonful of Bijol seasoning (gives the rice a nice yellow color)

- Don't know Bijol from Beans? Use Paprika instead.

- 1/2 pound of cubed ham or country ham cubed small

- One spoonful of adobo powder seasoning, if not available in Kansas, use salt and pepper. (See spice page)

- One 8 oz can of DelMonte's sweet peas

Ok, sounds like a hard dish to cook with a lot of ingredients, but once you get started, it's easy, trust me, it IS worth it. Let's go! You need a pot of course, where the heck else would you cook it? A deep pot 3 or 4 inches deep. If you are near a store that carries Puerto Rican or Cuban groceries, they may have a special pot for this dish. Pour the olive oil in the pot, rinse and dry the chicken first with a paper towel, sprinkle the chicken with the adobo powder or salt and pepper if this is not available. On medium heat, brown the chicken slightly, you don't want to cook it, just brown it, now throw the onions, garlic and cubed ham, stir with a wooden spoon. This whole process should take no more than 5 minutes. Now add water, enough to fully cover the chicken, cover the pot and bring it to a boil for about 10 minutes, throw the rice in, not from a distance or anything, just add the rice ok, stir again, add the rest of the ingredients (except the beer, sherry and the red pimentos) and mix well. Make sure the chicken bullion cubes dissolve well. Turn stove on LOW and cook for 40 minutes or so, have a beer, a cold Sam Adams would be just great about now, go back to the stove pour a beer and the sherry over the rice, spread the red pimentos on top, make it pretty ok, some kind of design if you want, and cover again, cook another 10 minutes or so. The outcome depends in part to the type of pot and the stove, this dish should be very moist, not soup, but very moist, if you taste the rice from the top and it feels a little hard, pour some more beer and cover again for another 10 minutes, don't burn it though! If you do...I'll come personally to your house and give you hell. This dish should be eaten right away. Have a fresh salad with it, good tomatoes, green romaine and olive oil with Balsamic vinegar, Cuban bread. The best side dish of "resistance" with Arroz con Pollo has to be "Maduros" (recipe later for these).

Everyone enjoyed the meal; food was consumed in good quantities and properly washed down with 3 bottles of Paternina Rioja which we happened to find at a large wine store in Atlanta. These were very happy times; the 3 Mosqueteers were at it again. Pilon brand Cuban coffee followed and that was topped with my bottle of the almond based liquor from Spain called "Licor 43" We walked out with our respective dates into a balmy Southern night and went down to a small lake nearby, Nancy was really impressed with the whole experience, she was a fun girl full of zest for life and good looks, life was good, Spain and my second year of medical school seemed like a distant thought as I produced my guitar (Ed, Angelo and I had formed a trio in college that performed in several campuses), a few words came to my mind which started to fit into the pattern of a song that turned out to be one of the best songs I ever wrote.

There are many stories about the summer of 76, which belong, perhaps in another book.

As August came to an end, the reality of going back to Spain to continue my studies hit harder than a middle linebacker for the Dolphins and before I knew it, I found myself in a plane over the Atlantic Ocean, sipping "Tio Pepe" brand sherry, heading back to Seville.

Don't worry my friends, there is more.

At this point, it seems like the right thing to do is to give you the recipe for:

4- MADUROS.

These are sweet plantains, not bananas! Plantains are bigger than bananas and meant to be cooked. They are imported from Costa Rica, Venezuela and other countries in Central America. As I mentioned before, sweet plantains are a must side dish with Arroz con Pollo. If you are reading this book in Montana, and have no idea what a plantain looks like or can't find them, well, just stick to the salad properly salted and peppered (my, I'm getting fancy!).

If you live in South Florida, plantains are easy to find, even in Boca Raton. So, go buy 6 or so and here is the catch, you need to buy them several days before you cook them, for they have to literally over ripe, they have to be totally BLACK outside, really soft, that is the ONLY way to cook them ok, got that? Let them ripe to that point, they also freeze very well if you have to save them; just put them in the freezer like that. Here we go, peel them by cutting both tips, making a longitudinal incision (ahh my medical terminology at work!), slice them at a 45 degree angle into sections and fry them in medium heat, it's best if the oil covers them. Fry until golden, I actually like the edges to be a little crispy and black. Fry them last, they are better served right out of the pan. A word of caution, plantains in the frying pan have built-in sensors that know when you walk away to get a beer or answer the door and they WILL BURN!, so, stay there, be a man and take the heat, watch them cook!!! They have to be turned unless you have a deep fryer and please, please do not use them for dessert, they are to be enjoyed with the food, take a bite of the rice and before you swallow, put a piece of that sweet plantain in your mouth, chew it together, it's a Cuban thing, they go with the rice and chicken like Batman and Robin, The Lone Ranger and Tonto, Starsky and Hutch or... You get the idea. I AM getting so hungry!

Around the summer of 77 to the best of my recollection, I had completed my third year of medical school and I was back home in Miami for some much needed R & R hanging around South Beach when one night I got a call from my old friend Leo. We go back a long time and there are many stories that could be told (or maybe not). Leo told me he was having a party for some of his friends and he wanted me to do the cooking since I had too much lazy time in my hands. He also mentioned as a way of enticement that among those friends there was a girl I should meet. I'm usually weary of blind dates and Leo reminded me of my mother and the many times she tried to introduce me to "nice girls". However my interest was raised when Leo mentioned that her father was a very famous Cuban musician and composer. Being a composer, guitar player, country-blues singer myself, I thought this might be fun so I accepted the invitation. Leo said he wanted me to cook "PAELLA". You got it, here comes the recipe. PAELLA is a very typical dish from Southern Spain, very similar to the Chicken and Rice, but it involves seafood and a fish stock base for the rice.

5-LA PAELLA DE NILDA (*Nilda's Paella*)

There are many variations to this dish, you can substitute, add subtract until you get accepted at MIT. I'll give you my version since I'm not MIT material. So, you need to go out right now and get:

- 2 pounds of medium shrimp with the skins and heads on (if they have no heads, get them at least with the skins on)

- 1 1/2 pounds of white fish, boneless and cut in chunks. Cod works great.

- 2 small cans of mussels from Spain.

- 1/2 pounds of clams, can clams are ok.

- One pound of cubed cooking ham (same ham you used for the Arroz con Pollo), well, not the SAME ham since you already ate that one I presume, I mean the same type of ham. Sometimes things need to be clarified in case there are some West Palm Beach voters.

- 2 pounds of Valencia style rice. The short grain rice. Same as... well ya know.

- The ingredients are very similar to the Arroz con Pollo, except this is a seafood base dish, so go get a bunch of Manzanilla pit less, pimento stuffed olives.

- 8 oz jar of red sweet pimento peppers. Goya fancy brand is very good.

- One large diced onion

- 4 large garlic cloves smashed or chopped small. A garlic press is very useful here.

- One 4 oz. can of tomato sauce (DelMonte, Diana, Goya)

- 20 hairs of Saffron, In South Florida, Badia brand sells them at a very reasonable price. Real Saffron is expensive, you can substitute it with Spanish Paprika (1 tablespoon)

- Bijol, one small tablespoon, this is for coloring, if not found around your neck of the woods, stay with the paprika or find some other rice coloring ingredient. I remember one time cooking this dish during of those "special" circumstances around 2 AM and not having any Saffron or Bijol, so after getting inspiration by a couple of beers, we used GREEN food coloring, maybe if had been St. Patrick's day it would have been more accepted. I do not recommend doing this, especially on a first date you are trying to impress. Oh, yeah, the rest of ingredients almost forgot.

• 1/2 cup Spanish virgin olive oil. (Sensat, Goya, Carbonell)

• 8 oz of dry white sherry

• One beer for you and save one for the dish

• One half tablespoon of salt and one half of Pepper, or, one spoonful of adobo seasoning (Badia or Goya).

How many people does it feed? Well, that depends on how much they eat doesn't it? Four good eaters of 6 wimpy eaters. Also keep in mind, you can use ANY seafood you wish, scallops, crab legs, lobster etc. Lobster tails work better cut in small one inch sections, crab claws are great here let's COOK! Boil the shrimp skins for 10 minutes, save it; this is the stock for the rice. A fish head along with the shrimp skins is even better. Yeap, the whole head, this is just to make fish stock. Most fish markets will give you heads for free, Grouper, Hake. Halibut, any fish head is fine.

In the same pot described for the Arroz con Pollo, pour the olive oil and on medium heat stir the onion, garlic, ham chunks and sauté for 5 minutes or so, pour the rice and mix quickly with the ham, onions and garlic .Pour water saved from the stock (without the head and skins of course, strain the stuff) until the surface is about an inch over the rice, throw the rest of the ingredients except the shrimp and the sweet red peppers. The shrimp should be peeled and deveined. Turn the stove on LOW, mix everything well and cover the pot, in about 40 minutes, check it, smell it, admire it, taste the rice from the top, it should be almost cooked, now, put the shrimp in, spread them around, bury some in the rice, pour the beer and a little more sherry, cut the sweet pimentos in small stripes, make a design, decorate this thing, cover and cook another 5 minutes. This dish should be very moist, like the chicken and rice. There are other variations for Paella, some will decorate with the sweet peppers and asparagus stalks, that's ok. I feel this is a pretty good version. If you want more flavor, salt and pepper can always be added at the end, better to be safe than salty. You do know that there are some things that do not go with this dish; sardines, anchovies, and imitation crab meat are OUT! I know what you're thinking (Clint Eastwood in "Dirty Harry"), too many ingredients, too complicated...NONSENSE! It will be fun and your guests will be very impressed. Of course you will encourage them to buy my book, have them get their own, I don't want you loaning them this book! So, let cook it, lets, do it baby, I'm with you in spirit, the force is with you!

Maduros is a must with Paella!!! Cuban bread, salad, and a couple of bottles of Paternina Rioja will add a great touch, want to go fancier? Try "Faustino's" Rioja. Beer is fine also, a very cold Sam Adams while cooking will cool the heat.

I hope you enjoyed the Paella. One thing that stands out in my mind about Leo's party was his mention of having just a "few" friends, so I figured cooking for 6 or 8 people would be fine, however as it turned out, there were 16 people there! Like the Marines say, I adapted, improvised and overcame. Upon the realization of the crowd size, my first thought was: "is there a pot big enough"? There wasn't one, I had to use two pots and split the ingredients in half, not an easy thing to do and two pots never come out the same. To collect my thoughts, I opened a cold Hatuey, a beer from pre-Castro days now brewed in Puerto Rico, started a Jimmy Buffet tune on a small cassette player in the kitchen, a while later while I was concentrating on the cooking and in the middle of adding some more beer to the Paella and my stomach, a voice behind me said: " Hi, I'm Nilda, can I help?" My friends, I have what I call "Fred's Rules", three of those rules are:

1- Never take a date to a Dolphin game, they usually get bored and ask dumb questions that interrupt my concentration. I don't just watch the game, I LIVE it.
2- Never take a date when I'm doing a music gig, they influence your concentration and besides, there are always plenty of girls you can meet after the gig.
3- DON'T let girls in the kitchen when you're cooking, they usually start giving opinions and stuff and they tend to get in my way.

Knowing those rules all my adult life, I finished pouring the beer on the Paella, turned around and said: I usually don't let girls in the kitchen when I'm cooking, but since you are so beautiful and I'm dying to meet you anyways since Leo told me about you, would you like to stay here for a while and pass me that jar of peppers?"
The night turned out great, The Paella was consumed in its totality! (My kind of crowd), beer and wine flowed over conversations from politics to medicine (never fails when they think you know stuff on your third year of medical school). Around 11.00 PM the crowd thinned a bit and we moved to the piano, her father played some of his original classic songs, what a talented musician! Of course, Leo opened his mouth and told them I also wrote songs, forced by the crowd (it really didn't take much at all), I played a couple of my original songs on a guitar that appeared as if by magic. Nilda complimented my songs and said something about the girls who motivated the songs being special in my life. I said they were in the past and only live in my music (quick response line, learn something here guys).
I saw Nilda a couple of times that summer. August was just about spent when I found myself in a plane going back to Spain for more medical school. She wrote a few times, I wrote once. Eventually I heard from Leo that she had

married a lawyer. The fact that she's part of this book means that a memory was kept, a nice one and that is all. The trajectory of a falling leaf determined by the wind.

AHHHH! Let's get back to food before you throw this book out the window!

6- ORANGE BOWL PINCHITO

I got hooked on this "pinchitos" when the Miami Dolphins still played their games at the Orange Bowl (hence the name). There is no particular story associated with this recipe but I decided to include it just for its pure goodness. Leo and I are avid Dolphin fans, during season, we would go to all the games, parking a few blocks from the Orange Bowl and walking to the stadium. There were many food vendors on the sidewalks cooking this pork shishkababs or "pinchitos", their smell was irresistible, by the time we made it to our seats, we had at least two and were finishing a third one with beer from the stadium. Before going back to Spain every summer, we would always catch a couple of exhibition games so one day Leo called me and said: "come over boy, game on TV, got beer" I replied: "sure thing man". The profoundness of that conversation was overwhelming. Beer, food, Football, it does not get any better than that... well maybe one exception. I decided to cook the pinchitos so we could get that "stadium" feeling. This is a man's dish, a football dish; "cool" women may enjoy it also. Here we go, go on out and get yourself:

- 1 1/2 pounds of fresh lean pork cut into small cubes about an inch thick.

- 2 or 3 limes, not lemons, limes ok.

- One tablespoon of salt, pepper and cumin powder all mixed well

- Bottle of sugarcane molasses.

- 2 oz of tequila, any brand, this is for marinating. If you plan on drinking it as well, Jose Cuervo gold does the job for me.

- One tablespoon of Spanish Paprika

This is easy, mix all the ingredients well and marinate pork cubes in the refrigerator for at least 4 hrs. Slice the cubes in a metal skewer, cook slowly on the grill until a dark golden color is achieved. Make sure you turn those suckers! If you don't have a grill, they can be broiled but it's just not the same. Have the grill on medium heat; you want to cook pork all the way through.

I was reminded as I downed the first one about those early September games at the Orange Bowl under very hot weather with the stadium literally vibrating under your feet from the stomping fans. I miss that stadium, thank God the University of Miami Hurricanes still play there and I can catch an occasional game. You can take the pork off the skewer and put them in a plate with salad etc. but they really taste better biting them off the skewer (careful here ok, don't puncture your mouth, that could ruin the ball game). The Dolphins now play at Joe Robbie or the so re-named Pro-Player stadium, modern, comfortable and not the same. Wash those pinchitos with a very cold Sam Adams or your favorite brew. Go Dolphins! Let me give you an example of what this pinchitos can do, let's say the Dolphins are down 4 points in the middle of the fourth quarter and Dan Marino throws a bullet between two defenders in the end zone and scores a touch down, you bite one of the pork cubes onto your mouth, the flavor fills you with gusto, the TV is loud and you hear the crowd screaming, you chew at a fast pace and then bring a frozen mug freshly poured with Sam Adams, take a big sip and let the brew wash down the bite of pork, life is all right, you high five and spill some beer on the rug, it's ok, there are no women present and besides, there is more beer where that came from. Get the point? Ok, as with the ingredients, you can substitute Dan Marino for your favorite quarterback and Sam Adams with your favorite beer, but... why would you?

7- SHRIMP CRAB CRIOLLO

Before medical school, I was working in the lab at Palm Springs Hospital in the great city of Hialeah, Florida. There are a lot of stories from this time period (Diane, Denise, hear that?), however that may be for another time. It was at this hospital that I met Francine, a smart, witty, fun loving girl with auburn hair and deep hazel eyes, sure, I asked her out and after a couple of dates she asked me to put my abilities to the test, cooking abilities that is since I had bragged about them so much. During a beach afternoon Francine asked me to go see some of the horses her father owned near the Hialeah race track, as we were looking at these beautiful animals, her father drove up in a mint, 1955 red Ford pick up truck. He seemed a very nice guy and was pleased to find out that my father had owned horses back in Cuba and as a child I often rode them; this created some important common ground between us. Of course, Francine had introduced me as "the guy who claims he can cook real good" and that prompted an invitation to cook at their house for his wife's birthday. There was no way out of that one.

The following Saturday I showed up at her house with some flowers for the wife and a cooler full of ingredients. More on Francine and that night later, for now, let's cook!

- 2 pounds of medium shrimp, peeled and deveined, get them fresh and do it yourself, none of that cleaned and frozen stuff.

- One pound of crab meat, if not found fresh, get it in cans, don't use the artificial stuff.

- One large green pepper thinly sliced

- 4 large garlic cloves diced small

- One handful (if you have a big hand, if not, use two handfuls) of fresh parsley.

- One tablespoon of Crystal brand hot sauce

- One 8 oz can of crushed tomato

- Salt and black pepper

- One large onion thinly sliced

- 1/2 cup of olive oil. You know my favorite brands by now.

In a large pan about two inches deep, pour the oil, on medium heat sauté the onions and green peppers for about 2 minutes, add the rest of the ingredients except the crab and shrimp, cook on medium low for about 5 minutes, add the crab and shrimp, mix well, cook for another 5 minutes. That's it, easy, serve with my basil tomato salad (recipe down the road) and white rice.

I introduced Francine and her parents to Marques del Riscal Rioja wine, a Blanc, served ice cold, fresh Cuban bread and I even brought my Cuban coffee maker for a deliciously aromatic Pilon brand Cuban coffee after the meal. Her father offered us a variety of liquors and I opted for Drambui, one of my very favorites. The night became mellow and I told her father about my childhood stories with horses and farms to which he showed genuine interest. Around 8.30, her father invited Francine and I to go with them and visit the art festival in Coconut Grove, I politely refused and told him this was THEIR night and they should enjoy it alone, perhaps take the wife to the Coconut Grove playhouse, treat her to a play for her birthday (not bad ha). I really liked Francine's parents and always felt the feeling was mutual on their part. Francine was an only child like myself and there were very good vibes between us. (for those of you in Rio Linda, California, "vibes" is a word from the 60's). Later, Francine and I went into their pool to witness a magnificent South Florida Summer sky. I thought of Jimmy Buffet and proceeded to the blender for that frozen concoction which turned out to be a Southern Comfort ice cone. Just crush the ice in the blender and add Southern Comfort, sip slowly with a straw. The water was perfect and warm, the reflection of a quarter moon made its presence known. I saw that look in Francine's hazel eyes, like an open book, like a newsflash on a New York marquise asking: "now what?" I held her body floating in my arms, kissed her quietly and thought about my next six years attending medical school in Spain, what were the chances for long romances...she knew of my plans...there was no need for further words that night.

After being in Spain for a few months, I got a letter from Francine. They had moved to Kentucky to raise more horses, one horse had become a good winner. A Christmas card came in my mail box that year with the words: "I'll never forget". It was cold, damp, and windy in Seville that day. I put the card in my pocket, got into my Fiat Spider and drove for a long time.

On a more humorous note, I was going to call this dish Francine's Crab, but somehow it didn't sound right.

I'd like to introduce at this time a section of the book called:

WISDOM AND SPICE

Quotes by me and other unknown sources.

"TRUE APRECIATION OF A MEAL STARTS WITH THE EYES AND THE NOSE"

"Never save a good bottle of wine for that special moment, bring that special moment to it"

"If your dinner date orders soda or ice tea with prime rib don't waste your time"

"If you make it to the second bottle of wine with your dinner date and she/he is still talking about his new car/her aerobics class, switch to Absolute or Stoly Vodka on the rocks with a twist, if the same topic of conversation persists, switch partners all together"

"People, who are wimps at the table, make lousy lovers"

"Life is a GIG"

"Never drink downstream from the herd"

"Illegitimi non carborundum"

This is a very important one: "If it didn't affect planetary rotation, it was not as important as you thought"

"Don't let anybody steal your dream"

"The day that you stop dreaming, it's the day you begin to die"

"If you can't hear, turn the amps up dude!"

I think you had enough wisdom for now, so let's get back to cooking.

8- CHICKEN A-1-A

A1A is referred to as the road that parallels the beach in most of South Florida. In South Beach it's called Ocean Drive, just a small geographical lesson to bring you back to the beach. I do not have accurate recollections about the night this recipe came about. I do know it was during one of the summers back from Spain while attending a Joni Mitchell concert at the Miami Beach auditorium. I somehow had scored a back stage VIP pass and was enjoying the end of the concert when a girl dressed in 60's hippy attire crossed my line of sight and sort of hung around near me, long straight blonde hair, blue eyes, tank top and old faded jeans. We sort of hung together and after the concert, I managed to speak to Joni (I called her that, it's Ms. Mitchell to you ok) on her way to the limo. I mentioned the true fact that I had once performed the same night at an old "coffee house" called "The Flick" in Coral Gables near the University of Miami (GO Canes!), and that I was actually in the same small warm-up room with her and not knowing who she was or who she would later become, established a conversation as we both tuned our guitars. This girl must have been impressed with that and invited me to visit a houseboat where she was staying. Her name...I don't recall as we drank a few beers, hunger stroke and I went to the small kitchen for it was time to cook: Chicken A1A.

- 2 pounds of skinless chicken breasts
- 4 cloves of garlic chopped small
- Handful of parsley. Chopped small.
- Handful of fresh cilantro if available. Chopped small
- Oregano
- Spanish paprika
- Salt and pepper (or adobo seasoning)
- Fresh limes
- Tyme
- Olive oil

Here we go, mix all the powdered ingredients along with the garlic. Pound the chicken breasts with a rolling pin or a mullet over a cutting board; make them as thin as possible. With you hands, yes your hands, rub the powdered ingredients including the garlic all over the thinned breasts. Smother them! get the stuff all over them, press it in. On a frying pan, pour olive oil, cover the bottom with a thin layer and fry the chicken on medium heat, turn it. They should be cooked until golden and almost crunchy outside but don't let them get too dry. Take them out and squirt a good squirt of lime juice over them. Want to have a veggie? Just open a can of DelMonte's summer harvest and heat it. This is a great dish.

We ate well and late that night, she and I, (what the heck was her name????), talked about the concert, downed a few more beers, another Florida night followed by a hot morning sun ended that recipe.

9- RAINY DAY CHICKEN SOUP

The summer of 78 finally ended and it was time again to go back to school and do another year of medicine in Spain. The trip back every summer brought a case of the blues to my soul, the thought of a whole year away from home weight heavy on me.

Arriving in Seville a thousand hours later (or so it seemed because of the time difference), we were greeted by a cold and rainy day, you guessed it already! The name of the recipe comes from...you know.

When I arrived at the apartment, my roommate Pablo was already there since he had taken a different flight out of New York. After unpacking my stuff and engaging in small conversation about our respective summers, we both realized we were hungry and not wanting to go out in that lousy day, I went to the kitchen where to my surprise, all the needed ingredients were there for an old faithful, mood elevating chicken soup. Are you ready? It doesn't have to be raining or cold to try this.

- One whole chicken, quartered and clean, chicken parts are ok. Leave the skins on and take them off later.

- 5 medium sized carrots, peeled and cut into 1/2 inch sections

- 5 cloves of garlic crushed of chopped small

- One tablespoon of adobo seasoning. (see spice page)

- One large onion, chopped in slices

- 3 cubes of chicken bullion (Knorr brand is great)

- 12 pimento stuffed manzanilla olives

- Handful of fresh parsley rinsed and chopped

- Handful of fresh cilantro (if you are in Nebraska, you're out of luck, just skip it)

- One large potato, peeled of course and cubed into one inch sections, or two medium potatoes, or 4 small potatoes, you get the idea)

- 6 oz of dry white sherry

This is really easy, one deep pot big enough for all the stuff, boil water and place the chicken parts and chicken bullion cubes in, cover pot, boil for 15 minutes, open pot (how else would you put the other stuff in?) and place the rest of the ingredients, cover again, turn to medium and cook for another 40 to 45 minutes. Take chicken out with one of those big spoons that has holes in it and place in large dish, careful, it is hot! Proceed to take the meat out with a knife and a fork, place clean meat back in the pot, and stir once. Add (important) a good squeeze of fresh lime to YOUR bowl and eat boy! One option that might be considered even though I don't think its necessary is to add a good portion of angel hair noodles during the last five minutes and bring to a boil, that's up to you.

Chicken soup does wanders for the soul and the body. I you grew up with Jewish parents and grandparents, you already know this. I had two big bowls and hit the sack, the sound of the plane still ringing in my ears, I thought about facing another school year and all the new situations it might bring, I started to drift into slumber with thoughts of South Beach, the Miami Dolphins (one of the hardest things to leave behind). Sleep finally took over my tired body and I went into limbo land with a dream of riding a huge wave...

10- COOL CAULIFLOWER MACARENA

The word Macarena has become somewhat popular due to that stupid song of the same name. Memories of ex vice-pres Al Gore trying to dance this song on TV during the Presidential election serves as a great example of ridicule. Macarena is the name of a church in the old part of Seville, Spain, this church keeps a statue of the Macarena virgin which as many other churches represented by different virgins, is guarded by a faithful group of followers who carry this enormous heavy statues during Holy Week on long processions throughout the streets of Seville, often lasting all night. These "carriers" of the Macarena are followed by hordes of faithful members of the church who are dressed in Roman outfits (For those is the left coast, this is Romans as in the time of Christ, not Armani suits). The size of the platform that holds the statue of the virgin must be at least 4o square feet, the statue at least 20 feet tall, adorned with jewels and gold, her tears are two pearls. This particular procession starts at midnight on Holy Thursday and is carried on the carrier's shoulders until 12 noon the next day. A "guide" sends signals to the carriers who are actually beneath the platform and unable to see their direction by striking a long wooden staff on the mostly cobblestone streets. At one point there is a famous stop before a low underpass where the procession stops and a woman dressed in a typical Andalusia (Southern Spain region) dress, comes out to the balcony and sings a "saeta", a deep Flamenco chant dedicated to the Macarena virgin which is heard in total silence by the crowd. It made my hair stand up; this is really something to see.

I wanted to give you a little background on the region; however it would take a whole long book to capture the culture and traditions of this region. I wanted to briefly take you out of the boundaries of this book, (food, sports, girls etc) in the hopes of capturing the interest of those beautiful, intelligent sophisticated female readers from New York, Boston, Philadelphia etc. I would consider this a great achievement since in spite of having been born in Cuba, I am more familiarized with the South, grew up mostly in Miami which during my teen years, had a very Southern flavor.

With all that out of the way, let's get back to the recipe and how that came about. I first tried this dish in a small tavern near the Macarena church. The concept of a "bar" or "tavern" includes for the most part a variety of small dishes called "tapas" and there are different specialties offered by all these small bars and taverns. I happened to stumble into one that looked crowded with locals, a sign of good food, after a few wines, I had made friends with the owner who's name was Paco. He brought a small clay dish for me to try his specialty, cauliflower. I loved the way he prepared it and asked him to bring me a few more. This "tapas" are small, but I'm 6.2, so I ate about 5 with a few more wines and by the time the night smelled the dawn I was Paco's close friend. Recipe:

- Go buy a large cauliflower right now!
- Virgin olive oil from Spain (you know the brands by now)
- A ton of diced garlic, I mean a whole large head, no kidding. Diced very small
- Balsamic or rice vinegar

• Salt and pepper

• Some paprika

Steam the cauliflower, do NOT kill it, make it at a point between crunchy to soft, more on the crunchy side. It will become easier if broken into 4 segments before steaming. Break it into small segments about one inch or so, no science here ok. Place them on a 2 inch deep glass serving tray large enough to fit the whole thing. Generously pour olive oil all over the pieces, Pour vinegar, and make sure they all receive a bath, easy on the vinegar, not too much. Spread the garlic evenly along with the salt, pepper and paprika. Cover dish and let it soak for a couple of hrs. Eat anyway you want it! Before a meal as a side dish, late night snack etc. This is actually a healthy dish, absolutely delicious!

I went back to Paco's place a couple of night later and we became closer friends, as I thanked him for sharing this simple recipe with me, he asked me for a favor and I said name it! Paco asked me if I could tutor his niece with her English once a week. I thought it might be fun to teach and besides, I could not say no to Paco and a day for the first lesson was agreed upon. Paco gave me directions to his house in the suburbs and on what turned out to be a beautiful spring day with the smell of orange blossoms permeating the air (this reminded me of home); I put the top down on my Fiat and headed for Paco's house. I found it without difficulty and arrived at a nice Sevillian style home with an abundance of colorful flowers all around it. I walked to the front door and knocked. When the door opened, I was greeted by a beautiful girl, long brown hair almost to her waist, deep green eyes and a wide smile capable of stopping the Man of Steel in mid flight. She was wearing genuine American Levy jeans and a black sleeveless top. My mind quickly rationalized that this must be the older sister of Paco's niece and then my heart went almost into ventricular fibrillation when she said, "hi, I'm Asuncion (common name in Spain), you must be MY English tutor" to which I responded after what seemed a year of silence: YES I AM! She asked me to call her Asu for short. THERE IS A GOD. Of course in the name of improving US-Spain relations, I proceeded with the first lesson right away. My mother always told me: "son, you should have been a Diplomat!"

For those of you non medical infidels, ventricular fibrillation means and electrical dissociation of the heart's conduction pathway affecting the ventricles, the left one if affected being the highest risk. If this condition is prolonged, it may lead to death. See, by now I had learned some medical stuff, it wasn't all food and girls.

There will be more on Asu later, don't worry, I won't leave you hanging. For now, let's go into:

11- CARNE CON PAPAS UFO (UFO Beef Stew)

I'll get to the UFO part in a second. This is not a dish to impress your first date; it's a dish for being hungry for real food, not made for the salad and pita, bottle water and sushi crowd from Beverly Hills or Boca Raton.

I have cooked this dish many times, but the one that stands out in my mind was in Spain circa 1977 during a UFO watch, yes my friends, you heard right (or more accurately, you "read" right). This was my third year of medical school in Sevilla and UFO's were still a very popular subject, besides, I am a very strong Trekker as in a Star Trek fan, not really called "trekkies" but "trekker". One night we had a few friends over the apartment waiting to start hitting the books for some exams coming up. Somehow, the conversation, properly fueled by a few wines, turned into UFO's. Someone mentioned she had seen reports in the press about UFO sightings at an electrical power plant next to a lake some 30 miles from Seville. This really perked our interest and we decided to visit this site and find ET. Packing a couple of bottles of brandy and Gin to keep us warm in this cold night (ah the medical savvy of properly trained medical students!) we headed out to the site where we finally arrived around 11.00 PM in the middle of a cold, star packed night. We parked under some trees on a hill a few miles off the main road where we could see the lake and had a clear view of the sky. Sitting on blankets and proceeding to consume some Brandy, many stories came and went and as the night got colder, I managed to cuddle close to one girl in order to conserve and produce more warmth, just following my US Army training. I noticed we were now working on the Gin and no one had reported a UFO, it was now about 1.30 AM so we decided it was time to return to my apartment. Upon arrival, we were all starving! And yes, here comes the stew! You'll need:

- 2 pounds of cubed beef, get a good cut or buy a couple of large steaks and cut them into one inch cubes
- 1 1/2 pounds of potatoes, peeled and cubed. Any type of potatoes will do but if you can find Creamers or small new potatoes, it adds a different dimension not only of sight but of taste.
- One large green pepper sliced.
- One large onion sliced
- 3 large carrots, peeled and sliced into 1/2 inch sections
- 4 bay leaves
- 5 garlic cloves, yes, five! Chopped small.
- One small can of tomato sauce
- One small can of tomato puree
- Salt and Pepper or one tablespoon of adobo seasoning
- Two beef bullion cubes
- 8 oz of red wine
- Olive oil

Here we go: In a large preferably heavy pot, add some olive oil, turn on medium low, with your hands, rub the meat with salt and pepper or with the adobo seasoning, place the meat in the pot and brown slightly, add the rest of the ingredients plus a cup of water, stir and turn to medium low, cook with patience for about two hours. I like my stew on the thick side, how thick do you want it? That depends on the amount of water you add. Stir it with a ladle before serving and dig in, DIG IN! MAN OH MAN! Real food for real man and women. A hunk of Cuban bread would be just right, what? No Cuban bread in Rio Linda? Any hard crust bread will do a good glass of Burgundy or Rioja will bring it down. Back to the story.

By the time we finished cooking, it was four in the morning, we all ate with gusto and most of the group crashed at the apartment that morning.

I woke up several hours later to a gray, cold and rainy Sunday afternoon dreaming of being aboard the Enterprise and facing battle with some alien spaceship. After a couple of aspirins, a hot shower and a cup of coffee, reality started to creep slowly back into my consciousness. I decided to head downtown (funny, when was the last time you headed downtown for something?) to see what the rest of the weekend would bring. By now you may be wondering, when did I study? We actually did study between these types of adventures; there was a lot of "cramming" just before final exams.

With a clean pair of jeans, my black wool sweater and a splash of Paco Rabanne cologne I got into my Fiat which to my surprise started on the first turn of the key. Pablo (my roommate) was still sleep, that guy could sleep for a whole day! I often checked for signs of life when he slept like that. Getting to one of our familiar "water holes" I ordered some a Cinzano sweet vermouth on the rocks, which always stirs your appetite and gets your body ready to eat. Believe it or not, I was a little hungry, so I asked foe a piece of Spanish omelet which in Spain is served in sections like a piece of pie, thick, tasty and loaded with potatoes. As I was biting the last forkful, a lot of our friends began to arrive and of course I did tell everyone that we actually DID see a UFO the night before and some actually believed the story and started to make plans to visit the site. Coffee was followed by a shot of Licor 43, I felt good, the gray afternoon drizzle was gone, it was still very cold but the night was still very young...

A lot of events occurred that year, some were great and some were not. My closest circle of friends as well as myself suffered from a lingering chronic ailment called "HOMESICKNESS" for the good old US of A. Pablo was from New Jersey, quite a few were from New York, another group including myself was from Miami and there was one crazy, funny Cuban-American from Kansas City named Felipe who could drink more than they could brew!

There were many American students in Seville that were not medical students who were exchange students attending an American college called Columbus College. Most of these students were of the female gender wanting to learn the culture of Spain. Needless to say, I fully believe in helping others achieve their goals and since already knew the culture fairly well from being there 3 years, I volunteered my services to the college for free so these students from Nebraska, Ohio, Indiana etc. had a better understanding of the culture. Ok, I tried to be serious, let's get back to food.

12- HAVANA BEANS DREAMING

During my return trips every summer I made it a point to stop for a few days at Rich Ventura's house in Long Island before connecting to Miami. Rich and I go back.....well almost back to Middle Earth, we served in the US Army together at a place called Ft. Polk in the middle of the Louisiana Bayou. Of course, this book could not fit all the stories from that time period, there were oh so many. After leaving the Army, the music and friendship lived on. Yes, we played music together in the Army, a group eventually called "The Folk Machine", our top performance being at a place called "The Pecan Club" but that is another story.

During one of my stays at Richard's place in New York, he had planned a party with guitars, blenders and crazy people, you get the picture. After many songs were played and many blenders were stirred with different versions of Jimmy Buffet's frozen concoctions, I decided to cook black beans for those who had never taste them. There were two large chickens roasting in the oven already. So, about black beans, you must know that they are meant to go with other dishes, like white rice and Cuban style pork. Do NOT call them "black bean soup", it's not soup. I was reluctant at first to call this recipe "HAVANA" since thanks to the sick monster that enslaves the island, only the privileged and the dollar paying tourists can see black beans along with other basic dishes that were once available to everyone and now are offered only to the elite and Communist party hierarchy. Ok, ok this IS a cookbook, but I could not help and try to enlighten some of you in the "left" coast.

Black beans go with white rice, and that combination goes great with pork and just about everything else, even fried fish. You will need...well, yes, black beans.

- One pound fresh black beans

- 1/2 pound of salted cured ham or bacon

- one large onion diced small

- Salt

- Olive oil

The secret here is slow cooking and soaking the beans overnight. If you do this, be aware, those suckers really grow and take up water. Rinse them once and discard the water, then in a large pot, cover the beans at least 3 inches past their top with water. Keep in refrigerator. Start coking at a medium-low temperature the next day. In a frying pan, fry some bacon and /or ham with the onion. When the beans are almost cooked (about two hours or more), throw the bacon / ham inside, add salt and cook for another 20 minutes, they should be very creamy and soft, not swimming in the water. At this point, add a tablespoon of good olive oil. Adding a green pepper to the onion when sautéed is also a good option. While you cook, have a couple of beers, watch the Dolphins on TV.

Back to Rich's party. I don't have much recollections from that night, I do remember that at one time Rich asked me something I don't' quite remember and I tried to answer him with a mouth full of frozen concoction which made me laugh and in turn shot a stream of the frozen stuff into Richards shirt reminiscing of a scene in the movie "The Exorcist". We finally proceeded to the chickens without forks and ate them in a manner that Henry VIII would have been proud. There were many nights at Richard's living room which became known to me as "The Well"

More on beans: If you are afraid of "gas" throw a pinch of baking soda as you cook them and that should work. If it doesn't work, just make sure that your friends are not "down wind" from you. Just kidding ya! Baking soda does work.

13- BASIL TOMATOES

There is no particular story attached to this recipe, really there isn't. I liked it so much I decided to include it in this book. It's simple, yet so delicious especially during the hot summer days.

You'll need tomatoes, no kidding!

- 3 or 4 large ripe tomatoes. Choose the best you can. If you have access to fresh vine ripe tomatoes, go for it.

- 6 large cloves of garlic, by now you know garlic rules!

- Salt and pepper

- Balsamic vinegar

- Virgin olive oil from Spain (I've mentioned the brands before)

- Fresh basil, a large handful

Slice the tomatoes in flat slices, not to thick and not too thin (that clear?)

In a large serving dish about two inches thick, place a first layer of tomatoes. Sprinkle salt and pepper to taste making sure all tomatoes are "baptized" well. Do the same with the olive oil. Preferably with a garlic press, cover all those red beauties well, don't be shy. Place a good amount of fresh basil making sure each tomato slice gets a share. Create another layer and repeat procedure. Do 2 or 3 layers. It's best when covered and refrigerated for a couple of hours. Serve with some good bread. This can be a meal in itself! Your taste buds will have an orgasm!

During the summer of 78 while being in Miami during my yearly break from medical school I had a chance to go to the Dominican Republic for some needed R & R. One of my very rich cousins has a place in the Northern Coast near a place called "La Romana" which is fast becoming the "Monte Carlo" of the Caribbean and a world famous golf resort. A beautiful place on top of a mountain that shows a magnificent view of a valley filled with Royal Palm and Coconut trees that edge a white sand beach with crystal blue water. Even paradise can get boring sometimes and after my third day of sun, rum, and pineapples I started to feel the need for some interaction with the opposite sex. So far, that had been zero, zip, nada... That Friday afternoon I was heading back to the club for some solid food when my eyes registered an image that sent my neuronal synapses into overloads of L-Dopamine. (See, I told you I had learned some medical stuff). This image could have passed for Bo Derek's double in the movie "10". I stepped a little closer to her and said "Hi", she said "Hi". The profound meaning of these eternal words made a permanent mark in our time continuum, cosmically speaking. After what seemed like eons, she said: "You speak English? And I said "You bet!" but if I didn't, I would learn it in a nano second (that's really fast ok, scientific stuff) just to get to know you.) I told her I was from Miami and was attending medical school in Spain, this trip being a mental health rehabilitation exercise. I invited Amy (her name) for lunch at the club and she graciously accepted. During conversation I found out that she was there basically for the same reasons I was, relaxation and getting away from the hospital in Miami where she worked as a nurse in the neuro floor. My outlook of this place had just taken a turn, same palm trees, same coconuts, same beautiful beach, same blue sky, now with the key ingredient that made the original paradise...paradise.

Amy invited me to meet her aunt who had retired in the island several years back and lived in a cozy old beach house with breadfruit and coconut trees overlooking the ocean. A place where one felt a sense of inner peace and calm. During that visit to her aunt's house, Amy and I spent most of the afternoon learning about each other while sitting on one of those two seat swings hanging from the porch, the Caribbean ocean in plain view. Jimmy Buffet's words from "Margaritaville" kept on coming back to me (Strumming my six string-on my front porch swing) when her aunt went into the Kitchen and I did hear a blender go off. It was all so fitting! A few minutes later her aunt placed a glass in my hand with that frozen concoction. My reaction after the first sip was to beg for the recipe which her aunt provided after some persuasion; here it is, just for you.

14- MANGO TANGO

There are probably two thousand variations of this drink; you can hardly screw it up. I really liked this one.

- Two ripe mangoes. Should you have a problem finding this in Kansas, use a large can of Dole Pineapple or DelMonte peaches

- 6 oz of white rum (Bacardi, Matusalem, Bermudez are great)

- 3 oz of Vodka (any brand ok here)
- 1 oz of Drambui liquor (Triple Sec, Grand Marnier ok)
- Half cup of sugar
- Ice

Simple, first, play Jimmy Buffets "Margaritaville", if using real mangoes, peel, slice the meat off and squeeze the pit with you hand in the blender (not while the blender is running for those of you in Rio Linda and West Palm Beach), place the rest of the ingredients in blender with as much ice as it will fit. BLEND BABY, BLEND. It should be like a smoothie, serve in pretty glasses and topped with a dash of Grenadine to give it a nice sunset effect. Straw, yes, just don't start trying to be cute and sticking silly umbrellas and things in the drink.

After disposing of a second blender of Mango Tango, Amy's eyes seemed to be a lot greener, we stayed alone in the porch feeling the breeze caress our suntanned bodies, the sun looked like a huge fireball perfectly balanced over the sea horizon, I knew it was a matter of time before it's fires would be put out by the ocean, we did not speak a word, there was no need as the din of the moment in all it grandeur played tricks with our minds. In the distance another sunset reflected on the water was interrupted by a sailboat, the night soon brought a million starts over us. Medical school seemed like a far away memory...

As the olds saying goes, all good things must come to en end, Amy and I had some very sweet and intense times in the island, but it was time to get back to the real world, hers in a hospital, mine back to Spain to try and complete medical school. We took different flights back to Miami. I wrote a song on a napkin on the way back and filed the past few days under "special memories". It was time to move on.

A note on mangoes.

Being of Cuban descent I have to recognize the fact that Cubans take mangoes very seriously, a sacred fruit to be eaten a certain way. It's one of the few things Cubans take seriously along with Cuban coffee, politics, jokes and romance.

Just before going back to Spain that summer, a trip to Kew West materialized out of the blue. I was enjoying a morning drive when my thoughts drifted (not a hard thing to do for me) and before I knew it I was on the road to the keys and getting close to the famous seven mile bridge where you can watch two oceans at the same time, the Atlantic and the Gulf of Mexico.

Key West is probably the only city that celebrates sunset every night with a street party, they also have the Southernmost spot in the continental Unites States (Texas makes this claim as well, but they are wrong). The street party was in full swing with all kinds of crazy people dressed in funky costumes. I started to get hungry (here comes the recipe) and let the smell direct me to a sidewalk café where I sat and ordered a Hurricane Reef beer, brewed in the keys. That brought a sign of appreciation from the waitress who instantly knew I was from the area. I asked her what was that great smell and she told me about the hose specialty which seemed a great choice that I now call:

15- SHRIMP AND CHICKEN SUNSET

- One pound of peeled and deveined large shrimp
- 1 1/2 pounds of chicken breast cut into one inch pieces or so
- A large handful of fresh cilantro
- Crystal brand hot sauce
- Tequila, for you and the recipe
- Salt and pepper
- One cup of mayonnaise
- Cup of lime juice

Fire up the grill! Rub shrimp and chicken pieces with salt and pepper very well, all over them using your clean hands. In a blender, mix all the other ingredients and have a shot of Tequila with salt to get your stomach juices flowing. Cover the skewers with the mix using a small paint brush. Make sure there is no paint on it (can never forget those readers from Rio Linda and Boca Raton, even West Palm). Place on the grill on medium heat and cook until it smells good! Chicken should be gold ok, make sure of that. Shrimp should be pink, don't let the shrimp dry too much. Keep on basting with the mix until it's cooked. Serve right out of the grill. This is sooo good!

The second Hurricane Reef tasted even better and was even colder. I enjoyed the meal so very much. Topped it with coconut ice cream and espresso coffee (not the same as Cuban coffee). The drive back to Miami was relaxing; the view of the ocean at night under a full moon was breathtaking. My time in Miami was running short for that summer. It was time to take the big silver bird back to Spain.

The trip back was uneventful, I slept most of the way waking up just to eat and drink Tio Pepe dry sherry. Back in Sevilla I finally resigned myself to another whole year in school. One positive note was the continuation of tutoring English lessons with Asu (remember her?) By now we had developed a very good friendship; her parents had accepted me as part of the family. Asu's father had a great sense of humor and always had a joke to share with me. They were so grateful for Asu's progress in the language of Mark Twain that often offered to pay me for the lessons to which I totally refused. Can you believe that? I would have gladly paid them to let me teach this incredibly good looking, witty, funny girl. One day her parents insisted on taking me to a Flamenco dance place. I love Flamenco music and quickly accepted the invitation. These places are called "tablaos", word coming from the hard wood floor where they dance. There were several "tablaos" in Sevilla, but most were filled with German tourists who didn't know Flamenco from Irish dances. This tablao though, was not a place attended by tourists but by locals. Amy's father teased me about this place and said I would stand out like a businessman in a three piece suit at a nudist camp since I am over six feet tall and long bleached blond hair. Asu used to call me "El Vikingo" (The Viking) since most Andalusians were dark skinned and short. I told him I wasn't worried and I could hold my own, I was used to attracting a lot of looks and often being spoken to in German by some of the locals who were surprised when I answered in Spanish and even with a decent local accent sometimes. Even my friends from the States were calling me Viking!

The night finally came and Asu's father insisted on driving. I sat in the front seat with him and his wife with Asu in the back, the Spanish way! Some of Asu's relatives were supposed to meet us there. We arrived at what looked like an old big house in the old part of Sevilla with its typical style consisting of a large outdoor patio in the center of the house. There were around 12 small tables on the tile floor and a wooden stage facing the tables. As Miguel (Asu's dad) introduced me to several people, I could almost sense their thoughts as they politely smiled and shook my hand but surely thinking about what was this "gringo" doing here? And how come he speaks Spanish so well? Even with some closeness to their local accent! I was used to all that. It's almost impossible for people from other countries to understand the concept of many different ethnic groups under the red, white and blue American frame. No other country in the world has such cultural diversification. People in that Flamenco club were in for a surprise that night. After consuming good quantities of a great local Fino (dry sherry) and seeing some really incredible Flamenco dancing and guitar playing one of the local guys who had been watching me probably wondering what's this German tourist doing sitting next to a girl like Asu (I'm sure those were his thoughts) and definitely with one Fino too many, approached our table and tried to drag me onto the stage to accompany the musicians with the traditional handclapping. This handclapping is an art form in Flamenco music that involves precise counter beats and intricate coordination with all kinds of syncopated rhythms. This guy had no idea I had gotten good at that during my last three years in Sevilla. Miguel tried to ward the guy off but I insisted to let him go and started to walk on stage as I downed the last of my sherry. Three minutes into the song, I had two female dancers smiling and doing turns around me. The stage was no stranger to me; all the different music gigs in every circumstance possible made us friends. That night brought one of those rare moments when you are performing and realize something bigger than you has taken control of the music (if you play music, you know exactly what I mean), I felt the music, became part of it, I could tell the guitarists were building into a crescendo, could feel the sweat of the female dancers next to me, the smell of Fino permeated the air and blended with orange blossoms. As the song ended, one of the dancers slid on her knee next to me and for a second there was absolute silence and that's when I heard Asu's voice in a low chant.. VI-KIN-GO, VI-KIN-GO, she was joined by her parents and relatives and then the stunned crowd followed. I knew at that moment I had become part of her family. I started to make my way back to the table and was met by Asu half way as she ran into my arms with tears in her eyes and gave me one of those kisses you never forget...

Where the heck are all the recipes? Don't worry, there's more coming your way. My relationship with Asu was never really defined, it was part romantic and full of fun, music, and wit, yet at times I felt like an older brother. I know she was one of the reasons my homesick blues were improved as I was often invited to eat with them and participated in their family gatherings. Being an only child, that was new and refreshing to me. We were close a couple of times, she had a way of calling me "mi Vikingo" that almost made me ask her to say that to me forever. For good or bad, I somehow held back, not an easy thing to do. Miguel (her father) had an exceptional understanding of human nature. One night after a few wines just between the two of us, he told me I would always be a son to him regardless of whatever happened between Asu and I. That lifted some pressure from my mind and once again I wondered what the fates had in store for me down the road.

16- SEMI-HINDU CHICKEN

Down the road happened circa the spring of 1978. A real tough year of medical school was taking its toll on my sanity, rehashing doubts about this whole medical school trip. Spring break in Seville was almost a month due to all the fairs and Holy Week celebrations. Ft. Lauderdale was out of reach and South Beach was even farther so I decided to travel places where I had not gone before, to seek new civilizations and boldly go where I had not gone before (theme from Star Trek to be played here). I purchased a Eurail train pass, changed strings on my guitar, packed some jeans and Dolphin shirts,, warm sweat shirt, my faithful sheepskin leather jacket, hard cheese, filled my leather wine pouch and took off to the Netherlands in search of true blonds! I believe to the best of my recollection it was somewhere between Belgium and Holland I decided to get some sleep in the train compartment since I was alone. The cabin was fairly comfortable and warm so I took off my jacket and used it as a pillow while the motion of the train acted as a huge dose of sleep medicine. I did not know where I was or how long I had been down in limbo when the sliding door of the cabin woke me up and a backpack figure walked in the cabin. As I was trying to clear the cow webs from my mind and see through the semidarkness of the cabin, a sweet female voice in what sounded like an unmistakably British accent said: "hallo, quite sorry to have awaken you". I may have been a tired, hungry and weary traveler, but I became fully awake, realizing that this trip had just taken a turn into a whole new dimension of sound but off sight, the sight of long straight black hair, light olive skin, and deep blue eyes. Rod Serling would have been jealous! I offered to help her with the backpack and after a brief introduction and small talk I offered her some chocolate thinking of the GI's in WW II. "I'm really glad you chose cabin since I was getting quite lonely" I said. She smiled and said "very pleased to meet you, my name is Eva. (I thought about Adam of course but did not pursue the joke). As she straightened out her long hair, I though of how a woman can say worlds with a stroke of her hand and how inadequate we men feel sometimes when we try to express a small feeling with a thousand words just to fail miserably at it.

Only a few minutes had transpired since Eva had entered my life and I thought, of all the countries and trains in the world she had to come to this one at this specific moment in time, to this specific cabin (ok, I stole a little from Bogart in Casablanca).

One hour and 26 minutes later I knew more about her and her about me than many old married couples. Eva's mother was from India, her father was a British attaché at the British embassy in Bombay where he had met his wife. Eva (another twist of fate) was also a Medical Student in London and was initially a bit incredulous that I was a medical student in Seville. Why Seville? She asked. My answer: "It was dictated in heaven a long time ago that I would study in Seville, decide on seeing Europe this particular spring and chose this train, this particular cabin so we could meet somewhere between Sweden and Belgium" Eva smiled and made some comment about typical American ingenuity being alive and well in this train. I can not possibly go into all the details of that trip from that point on, suffice it to say it was as close to a movie script as one can dream. We spent the rest of our spring vacations traveling together, cuddled in dark train cabins, forgetting the world outside and not caring about a sense of time and reality. The time came however to end the trip and go back to our respective medical schools. I did not know how to categorize this encounter yet, there was no doubt Eva had made a strong impression in my life. I went back to Seville to face a month of hard cramming for final exams. After this massacre, I found out the entire special cheap charter flights we normally took back to the states were full and I was close to broke. The prospect of staying in Seville through the summer with all my friends gone back to the states was a bleak one. A couple of days later and with final exams behind me, my mind felt like a bowling ball was bouncing on the few brain cells I had left. We all had mailboxes at the post office and I went to check my mail that morning and found a yellow slip that indicated I had some registered certified mail. As Turning the slip into the proper window I received a thick envelope and the first thing that caught my eye was the stamps indicating the envelope came from England and everything started to unfold with joy as I realized it was from Eva! Inside there was a note that said: "I hope this reaches you in time before you return to America for the summer. Love, Eva" with the hand written note there was a plane ticket Seville-London (with a 3 day stay)-Miami. SOMEONE LIKES ME UPSTAIRS!

As I arrived to Heathrow Airport and finally cleared my bag and the Martin D-12-20 (my guitar for those of you non-musical folk) a familiar voice called my name. The British are not usually known for their affectionate displays in public but that costume was shot to pieces as Eva rushed and embraced me for the longest time, I did hear a comment from one of the exiting passengers that said "must be an American chap".

After some words and a few more hugs I noticed a gentleman watching us who introduced himself as Nigel I a very formal way, even called me "sa". Eva said he was part of her family's staff and he would be driving us home. I reluctantly let Nigel carry my guitar just to be polite. Once in the car, (an older immaculate Bentley Aston-Martin)

I started to feel a little uneasy and shot a bunch of questions to which Eva responded: "you Americans are always curious about everything" to that I replied: "yeap, that's how we invented Coca-Cola, Rock and Roll and got to the moon" We both laughed and she started to fill me in with details during the almost two hour trip back to her house. Eva said how much our meeting had meant to her and how much she had missed me, to the point that it had affected her final exams, a fact her father insisted she explain. (I can just hear her saying: I met this guy in a train who claims to be a medical student etc etc.) Her father had insisted in meeting this young man who had made such an impression on her daughter! After digesting the implications of this revelation, I felt a hint of fear in the epigastric region, and thought about jumping from the car but it was going too fast and I could not leave my guitar behind which was in the "boot" (the trunk) so I decided to face the old man.

All my fears were totally unfounded as it became clear later that her father just wanted to meet the young man from America whom he had heard so much about. I was really ready to face him thinking of a vision between Winston Churchill and Margaret Thatcher all in one package. I would make my country proud! All the way, USA! (Crazy ha?)

As we arrived at this big old house, more like a castle, a friendly warm voice greeted me by saying: " young man, I am most delighted to meet you" and I knew right then and there I would be jusssst fine.

Eva's father looked like a character from a Rudyard Kipling story, white hair, strong and sun weathered, handle bar moustache with deep blue eyes (I knew where Eva got hers). His wife also came out to meet us, a very beautiful woman with very soft Indian features and a kind gentle manner obviously very well educated. I developed an immediate liking to them and had the sense the feeling was mutual. Had fate finally caught up with me? Was this my future? Well, you'll have to read on and keep in mind this IS a cookbook ok? Recipe is coming here very soon.

I was shown into the guest quarters and told by Nigel dinner would be served at 7.30. After a shower (warm water, only in America do you take for granted really hot showers) and shave I took out a pair of dark dress slacks, a light blue long sleeve dress shirt and fully socked penny loafers since I knew this was no blue jean and sandals dinner. Soon my nostrils were filled with a delicious aroma and I realized I was really hungry. We al sat at the table and enjoyed a truly magnificent dinner full of stories from my life and their lives over a rare Chianti reserve from Ruffino. Of course my culinary abilities were included in the stories (sans the characters of course) and I inquired as to the way the chicken was prepared that night. I have never been able to truly duplicate it but it comes close. Here you go:

- A section, about an inch of Ginger root or half a cup of Ginger powder, fresh is so much better.
- Juice of two large lemons
- 8oz of DRY vermouth. Cinzano or Martini & Rossi
- Half a cup of curry powder. Curry can go from mild to hot like the surface of the sun. It's up to you.
- Two eggs beaten (but not defeated)

- Four large leeks or green onions. Shallots are ok.

- Four chicken breasts (more if you have more people of course, or if you want doubles.

- Peanut oil. Not olive this time. If you don't have peanut, use sunflower.

- White flower

- One tsp of salt and one of pepper

In a tray about one inch deep, mix the flower, curry powder, salt, pepper. Dip the breasts in the egg mix and cover with powder mix and set aside .Pour oil in a frying skillet until bottom is covered with thin layer. Throw the fresh Ginger in (from a safe distance, not from across the kitchen) and mix with oil. Do not turn stove on yet. If using Ginger powder, do the same, throw the green onion, and place chicken breasts in skillet and turn on medium heat. Watch them, you will turn them after about 6 minutes, they should be golden and almost crunchy outside. When cooked, take them out of the skillet and pour Vermouth and lime juice on the skillet with the other stuff left in it, mix well, this will make sort of a light gravy you will pour over the cooked chicken breasts. Decorate with slices of lemon and parsley garnish on top, serve with white rice or baked shallot potatoes. Enjoy!

Dinner with Eva and her family went very well in spite of a totally different setting for a South Beach soul. Life does throw a different scenario once in a while. Enjoy the moment for it may be fleeting and may never come again.

In the next two days we visited some of the local pubs and shops nearby and went into the city where she Eva took me to the usual tourist spots. I always had the strange feeling that we were being watched, something really not out of realm of possibility due to the fact of her father's admitted past connections with the intelligence community. No, his name was not Bond!

On my last night at her house, we held long conversations while holding hands as we walked through the gardens around the house. We embraced and kissed as the corner of my eye caught movement on a second floor window curtain. My resistance and control were comparable to soft Jell-O in a summer night, the words rolled out of my mouth like a Rocky Mountain snow avalanche. Words like the big: "I love you" and stuff like that.

I did not sleep well that night. Morning came with a bitter-sweet taste, the thought of leaving and the wish to stay. Nigel placed my things in the big Bentley and drove us to the airport. Not much was said between us but the moisture in our eyes spoke worlds. I finally boarded American Airlines flight 1701 non-stop to Miami, again before boarding we kissed as long as we could drawing comments from an old couple: "look at them Sam, they must be in love"

Eva had never pressured me for any kind of commitment. I told her I would write her a long letter as soon as I got back to the states and collected my thoughts. She had expressed in a very romantic way that no matter what the future held, there would always be a very special place for me in her heart. I said more or less the same thing to her and was engulfed by the belly of a 747. After take off I asked the stewardess (ok now they are called flight attendants but I am not politically correct) for some heart medication. Her look of concern turned into a sweet understanding smile when I explained and a minute later a double shot of Old Grand Dad on the rocks was in my hand. This treatment was used PRN and eventually Orpheus got a hold of my body and turn the day into slumber. I was awakened by the sound of the landing gear at MIA

(Miami International Airport), I was home at last, at least for the summer.

I always thought that everyone should have somebody waiting upon arrival at airports, train stations etc. It should be an option provided by the airlines or travel agencies. One could request some kids and a wife, a pretty girl, parents or just a group of friends who would hug you and say welcome home, we missed you! A professional greeting service, an idea who's time has arrived??? (get it? "Arrived"). This was not the case as I arrived at MIA that day on a hot, humid and overcast day. On the Yellow cab, the driver from Havana said with great eloquence: De ercondicion es broque, which translated means, the air conditioner is broken. As we headed on the Dolphin expressway to my parent's house I noticed a billboard advertisement on the side of the road that said: "Fly to London with us, British Airways will take care of you." I closed my eyes and drifted in thought until the taxi stopped.

IT'S TIME FOR A LIGHTER NOTE, SO, HERE IS SOME:
FOOD FOR THOUGHT, OR PERHAPS IN THIS CASE, SOME THOUGHT FOR FOOD!

A meal is not just the act of feeling the body with nutrients; it should be a profound experience with roots dating back to early man gathering around the safety of fire after a hunt. Millions of stories have been told over a course of a meal. Plans for war and peace, prelude for romance, promises made. The last thing a condemned man gets is his favorite meal. Jesus spoke of his betrayal and his remembrance during the most famous meal in history. Caveman ate and stared at the stars in awe and fear of the night after a meal. Today, we still light candles for special meals, sit around a piece of wood and speak of the day's experiences and possible challenges of tomorrow. Has it really changed much in the last few million years? In cosmic time it's really a second.

Ok, this is as deep as I'm going to get.

Being back in the states provided a chance to reflect on the events back in London and I was able to shake some cobwebs from my mind. That summer I worked as a doorman at the Columbus hotel in downtown Miami, money was good thanks to the tips and I was able to get out in time everyday to take a short drive to South Beach and enjoy the late afternoon hours. One day I received the usual call from my friend Leo (Remember Nilda's paella?) to see if I wanted to cook again for some friends. Same conversation occurred, got beer? Sure thing. This brings us to:

17- OSO BUCCO A LA SAUECERA

- 6 large veal shanks. As lean as possible. If they are small, get 12.

- One large onion diced (or 2 medium, 4 small and so on)

- Eight, yes, eight large garlic cloves smashed in a mortar with salt

- One tablespoon of Oregano

- One 16 oz can of DelMonte's fresh cut tomatoes

- One small can of tomato puree (Hunt's ok)

- Two spoonfuls of Spanish Paprika (Pimenton), Badia is good

- Two tablespoons of Adobo Badia (see spice page) or salt, pepper, cumin mixed.

- 4 bay leaves

- One large green pepper sliced thin

- One tablespoon of Crystal brand hot sauce

Let's cook!

In a large heavy pot pour some olive oil, enough to cover the bottom of the pot with a thin layer, rub the shanks well with adobo/or salt and pepper and the smashed garlic, place the in the pot and brown slightly on medium heat (both sides). Add the rest of the ingredients and 9oz of dry white sherry. I know what you might be thinking, I didn't add the sherry in the ingredient list, well Huss, I forgot. By now you should know I love to cook with sherry. You have no excuses for not having a good dry sherry like Tio Pepe. Have a glass while you're cooking the shanks, make sure is the right sherry glass and the sherry is chilled properly. Sip it slowly. Cover the pot and cook on medium low for an hour and a half. The shanks should be fork tender.

Leo's party went well, this was a new set of friends I had never met. Dinner was served with white rice and sweet plantains (maduros!) preceded with a salad made of greens, water crest, sliced tomatoes and Vidalia onions all dressed with Sensat olive oil, balsamic vinegar and Goya salad seasoning. All with help from a few bottles of Marques Del Riscal Rioja. I went over some of my most recent stories from Spain which brought a remark from a doctor who had attended the University of Miami who said he must have gone to the wrong medical school. By the way, when you use hot sauce as indicated in some recipes, don't burn the dish by making it Mexican, Cuban cuisine (where many of the recipe's stem from) has its roots for the most part in Spain where only in a few rare occasions "hot" spices are used. Cubans using hot spices may be a misconception from the left coast.

Summer was going to fast as usual, June was closing its last few days and that meant the 4th of July would soon be here. One of my favorite holidays, not just for the usual fireworks and great food on the grill, but for what or represents. We often take so much for granted and tend to forget all the sacrifices done by so many to preserve our way of life. Many of the signers of the Declaration of Independence lost all they had and suffered even torture to their sons and never compromised their ideals. There is a great detailed article by Rush Limbaugh's father which was re-printed in Rush's newsletter sometime back that brings so much clarity to that issue. Strongly recommended! GOD BLESS AMERICA!

July went fast, my job at the hotel produced some needed food for my wallet. I had managed to spend a good amount of time at the beach, my tan was good, and my hair was 2 inches longer and 5 shades lighter. Just when I was beginning to feel at home in my God given natural habitat, it was time to return to Spain for what seemed my tenth year of medical school.

In case you paid attention to the previous section, I did write Eva and told her of my wish to perhaps see her again, travel to London on my way back or during my Christmas break. It all seemed so far away... I tried to arrange a flight connection back to Spain via London, it just wasn't possible. I wonder if I just didn't want to or tried hard enough.

One thing I wanted to do before returning to Spain that summer was to cook the eternal, traditional, legendary, Cuban style pig at Leo's house. My parent's place was too small. Leo agreed, I told him though, this would not be his lawyer crowd but more of a beach crowd.

18- LEO'S PIG WITH MY MOJO WORKING!

The day finally came and I was at Leo's house early to prepare the stuff. This was going to be BIG. We had an 80 pound pig which we got from a farm that sell's the pigs cleaned and ready to cook. They grow them on natural stuff, running around. That makes a great difference on the taste. Leo's grill was big enough for the animal, I made a gallon of mojo, Cuban style marinade (recipe in the back) and actually bought a ton of black beans, maduros and yucca (also known as Cassava). Along with Chicken and Rice, this menu is like the National Anthem, it's a must for all Cuban descent citizens, even if they were born here and became Boca Yuppies, the smell of the cooking pig brings all the roots back just like the sound of "tumbadoras" (Conga drums). We had two large coolers full of Coors plus a large batch of home made Sangria. Miami in late August, 91 degrees, clear blue skies without a cloud, slight breeze, the smell of a roasting pig and a clear blue pool, Jimmy Buffet coming loud and clear with (ironically) "Changes in Latitudes", how appropriate for my last week in Miami! What else is there I ask? Linda, Denise and Diane pulling in the driveway, that's what. My friends from the surfing crowd in their tanned, bikini clad bodies that had arrived early to help me cook (how nice). I overheard Leo's wife asking him who had invited those girls and Leo telling frantically they were MY friends and he had never seen them before! (That was funny). I took a large swallow from my Coors and dipped in the pool. GOD I love South Florida!! I could not believe that in just a few days I'd be back to the cold, old, cobble stone streets. For now, I pushed it out of my mind and concentrated on the pig, yeah, the pig, don't burn that sucker. The pig was properly marinated with the mojo; a variation can be used by rubbing the whole pig with salt, a ton of fresh garlic, some oregano powder and bitter oranges (limes if bitter oranges are not available in Montana). By the way, you don't have to cook a whole pig; this also works with a fresh leg.

I had to make sure this pig came out right. One reason, Leo's mom was there. She loved me like a son.

The key to this cooking affair: TIME, it has to be cooked slow, a pig that size may take up to 6 hrs with the grill lid closed. Leo had a grill made out of a 50 gallon drum, we made sure there was plenty of charcoal and the right heat from the ambers. Check it often and make sure the heat is there! Pork should be cooked well; it should fall off the bone. Baste it with mojo once in a while.

After many beers and dips in the pool we were ready to eat, the table was set outside by the pool, the taste was totally indescribable. Denise and Diane's bodies were further darkened by the sun. Everybody had some words of wisdom for me, persevere and finish, we'll be here when you come back next summer. Leo's mother however told me my true place was on stage with my music. She knew me better than my mother. Damn, that stage does fill me so... The sun had shed its last rays and the night had introduced an army of stars. We cleaned up the area when the party had died down, later Diane asked me if I wanted to go to the beach for a walk, she had perceived my feelings with the closeness of the return trip and wanted to help clear my head. As we walked in the still warm sand, the full moon bathed us in an eerie glow. Diane was so tanned her teeth looked like white pearls. We walked and spoke about our surfing days and how we all had to grow and face some responsibility and how many of our friends thought it was nuts for me to go to medical school (more words of wisdom). The moon over the Magic City of Miami smiled at us and later blushed a little with our kiss...It was time to go back to Spain.

One nice thing about flying Iberia Airlines back to Spain is that you can drink all the Tio Pepe sherry you want as courtesy of the airline. Tio Pepe was doing a god job at destroying some brain cells containing certain memories that were not wanted at this time. I tried to read one of Clive Cussler's books in which the main character, Dirk Pitt was trying to raise the Titanic and uncover a deep mystery. Tio Pepe finally won its battle and I felt sleep dreaming of the Titanic being raised to the surface. I have always been a light sleeper and when a change on the sound of the engines occurred, I woke up realizing we were beginning our descent on Madrid's International Airport.

My neck felt stiff and my Sternocleidomastoid muscle (Anatomy, second semester, lesson 4) was in pain. I asked the stewardess for some tomato juice and three aspirins, she gave me an understanding smile and was back a minute later with the goods. A few minutes later I seemed to be re-joining the world of the living medical students. My ears began to pop as the plane started its final approach, I could see the airport in the distance but to my surprise, it was left behind as the plane seemed to climb past it. Having flown often, I knew this was not normal and suddenly I was fully alert, my adrenal glands started to pump epinephrine into my blood stream. The captains' voice cane over the intercom with an overly calm tone ands said we were having a "minor" hydraulic problem with the landing gear to which I thought: "minor problem my gluteus maximus! There are no minor problems on a plane in flight, they are all major! One more approach was tried without success. I started to think about some of the situations described in Cussler's Dirk Pitt adventures and actually began to feel a little excited at the prospect of an emergency landing without the landing gear! (How stupid can that be). Finally after a very loud "thud" that caused sort of a mass scream from the passengers (except me of course), the landing gear was released and we landed at Barajas Airport. My first thought was the prospect of seeing Eva again.

After going through customs, I took a domestic flight to Seville and during its 53 minute duration, became acquainted with Alicia, one of the stewardesses. Alicia was tall for a Spaniard, long brown hair, olive skin and sensual green eyes (those Moors left their seeds all over Spain). Alicia agreed to have dinner with me after our arrival in Seville, we were both starved. She had her car at the airport, a spacious Peugeot 404 that fitted both our luggage with room to spare. I suggested we go to "Rafaelo's", the only true Italian restaurant in Seville. The owner (Rafaelo) was a good friend of mine and I had often taken several dates to the restaurant where he delighted in providing special service and always made it a point to compliment me on bringing beautiful girls to his restaurant. Rafaelo always said I reminded him of his younger days.

By the time we got to the restaurant the crowd had diminished somewhat, Rafaelo welcomed us with a big hug and asked me about my summer vacation. He started to mention something about my last visit and what had happened to that beautiful girl when he realized my eyes were shooting a death ray into his heart and apologized to Alicia who didn't seem to really mind since we had just met. He finally said" and who is this beautiful lady in an Iberia Airlines uniform?" I introduced him to Alicia and told him we were starved. He apologized and directed us to a nice table and told us not to look at the menu, he would take care of it. I trusted him and after a bottle of a special Umbria region Blanc reserve appeared on the table as if by magic, Alicia and I toasted to our very new friendship. The wine tasted good and took the edge off. Soon the smells from the kitchen increased the awareness of our hunger. A second bottle of wine was ordered when the food arrived. I got the recipe from the chef days later so I'll call this:

19- ALICIA'S LINGUINI

- One pound of medium shrimp peeled and deveined. I hope you know what I mean by "deveined" since this computer thinks of it as an error and throws that stupid red line under it. Just in case, deveined means taking out that black stuff from the dorsal aspect of the shrimp, take a sharp small knife, hold the shrimp firmly and slice across the body under running water. There, it's covered. Do I need to tell you how to take the skins off? C'mon, I hope not.

- 1/2 pound of scallops

- 1/2 pound if clams (cans are ok)

- 1/2 pound of mushrooms, rinsed and sliced thin

- Yeap, more garlic! About 6 cloves sliced thin

- One large onion chopped small

- Large handful of parsley. I hate it when I see other books and TV cooks calling for 1/2 cup of parsley? Hell, put some in there! Big hands are ok!

- Salt and pepper. Use your taste and judgment.

- Olive oil (you know the brands by now)

- 4 oz of dry Vermouth

- Linguini, one pound. I like Barilla even though it takes a little longer to cook. Other brands are ok. Boil in large pot; put them in slowly at full boil, water should have a little oil and a pinch of salt. Some people like pasta "al dente" which is a little harder, almost chewy. I like mine well cooked, not mush, but cooked all the way. How long? Check the box for instructions.

While the pasta is cooking, in a large skillet, pour olive oil, throw onions and sauté for a few minutes until onions appear clear, throw the rest of the ingredients except parsley and Vermouth, cook on medium heat until shrimps look pink. This is a good sign they are cooked. Stir all the ingredients well. Add some more olive oil, maybe a tablespoon, maybe more. Add the Vermouth and parsley, stir again and cover for two or three minutes. When the pasta is ready, drain well and pour skillet mix over it, serve in individual plates with a good hunk of crusty bread and pour some more wine on your glass. Take the first bite, push it with bread and wash with a good sip of wine. Enjoy the moment, enjoy life.

We followed the dinner with coffee from Portugal and my favorite Licor 43. After thanking Rafael for such a wonderful dinner, Alicia insisted we go for a walk on the riverside area. The Guadalquivir River is a very historical river. Chris Columbus made port here after his trips to the Americas. There is a famous tower overlooking the river called the "Torre Del Oro", (The Tower of Gold" which was used as a customs building where the gold and other goods brought from the New World were counted and taxed. Man, history at my feet! This was a very romantic area where orange trees perfumed the air with their blossoms, benches where couples could sit and look at the water. This was one of my favorite areas of the city. Many open air restaurants were found here. There was a definite special feeling to this area. We took a long walk and somehow her hand found mine. Her apartment was nearby and she had mentioned the view of the river from her window was magnificent, I agreed to check her...ups, the view I mean. The apartment was small and cozy; it DID have a great view of the Tore Del Oro. The opened window brought some faint late night sounds from the street and the fragrance of Jasmine she had growing in pots on the balcony. The moon threw us a curve, the reflection on the water was like a narcotic and the rest of the night became intimate.

The sun brought the sounds of the city to my senses around eleven AM. As Mr. Spok (Science officer aboard the USS Enterprise, Captain James T Kirk Commanding Officer) would say, the most logical thing to do at this time was to have breakfast so Alicia and I showered away the smells of the night and headed out to a cafeteria where they served a very special soft bread called: "Pan de Gloria"(Glory Bread). I remembered this bread from my childhood, it was the first time I had seen it since. We ordered coffee which was strong and excellent, Portuguese for sure and some of the sugar covered breads. I devoured a few and the coffee felt good in my belly. The strong coffee started to fire more L-Dopamine across my brain synapses (in non medicaleese, I started to think more clearly). Alicia was flying back to New York the following night and wanted to shop for some typical Andalusian items for her friends in N.Y. She invited me and I came along, it was the best "first day back" I had ever had when coming back from the states after summer vacation where it would usually take me a few days to get acclimated. Later that afternoon in a rare moment of sanity I realized I had to get my things out of Alicia's apartment before she left again or this would turn into a more permanent arrangement. My roommate Pablo was already wondering what had happened to me since I didn't show up at our apartment the day before and he knew I was due back that day. He really was not too concerned, Pablo knew me well by now.

Alicia was great, had a good sense of humor, was very attractive and spoke English well, did not seem ready to start a serious commitment, knew the city very well, all great points but I had another year of medical school ahead of me, time for the task at hand, time to move on.

Fall came and went very fast that year, December brought the cold winter showing no mercy on this tropical guy. After a couple of hard exams I decided it was time for the Viking (the name had stuck) to go north and explore the Basque country. The narrow roads and snow covered mountain paths made for a refreshing change of scenery. The quiet drive, interrupted only by the Fiat's engine pushing through the snow covered mountains opened my mind to a recollection of thoughts and experiences during these last few years since attending medical school. Being in the middle of nowhere without anyone knowing of your whereabouts is a situation that I feel must be explored by everyone. It lets you "hear" your own thoughts and often helps answer pondering questions with simple answers previously overlooked. This was a breathtaking ride attended by God, me and the mountains! When a small town did cross my way, I made it a point to stop, taste the local wine and meet new people. Many miles into the trip through the Alps, I crossed the French border, I wanted to visit the French Northern coast and maybe see Normandy and all those beaches made famous during D-Day in World War II. I needed to see the ocean, even if it was cold. The snow suddenly increased and visibility became almost zero. Where did the wrong turn occurred I don't recall as the snow seemed to coming from all sides now. I was thinking if the Dolphins had made the playoffs when the road seemed to disappear from under me and it became very bumpy. I started to sense something was wrong when the site of a cow barely a couple of feet from the car made me swerve and almost loose control. I managed to stop, it was almost dark and the realization of being lost struck me like a hungry linebacker on a quarteback and I realized I was no longer on the road...

For a second, an ironic thought came to mind about being stuck in the snow and freezing to death after escaping Castro's Cuba as a child and serving in the Army during Viet Nam! I could have been killed when years back Leo and I dove off Government Cut in the middle of the night just to impress some girls from Ohio, or when I was hit by a heavy surfboard right on the nose and the day went black, voices were far and a thousand points of light appeared in front of me. The thought of dying by freezing somewhere in the middle of the French mountains dissipated and logic started to fill my brain cells. I had some food supplies with me, a couple of Pears and some wine; I could survive the night if I had to. Trying to get some direction I got out of the car, put on my old faithful sheepskin jacket and tried to get my bearings. After a few minutes I found the road but the snow was falling hard and I didn't think the low riding Fiat could make it back to the road. I always carried road flares and decided to light a couple and put them on the road. My prayers were answered by a set of approaching lights that seemed to be slowing down. A truck finally stopped and after explaining my predicament to the driver between my limited French and his poor English I was offered a ride to his nearby house. We would come back for my car in the morning.

The house was a typical French country house and it had adequate heat, a rare thing in Europe, at least for this Florida boy. I helped Jackes bring some things from the truck inside. His wife welcomed me and seemed very friendly. From what I was able to understand, he explained to his wife about picking up a crazy American tourist driving a small sports car on the mountains in the middle of a snow storm, she laughed and gave me a compassionate look and started to pour some Cognac. Now, I know what you're thinking, the man had a daughter and etc etc. This time that was not the case. They did not have any kids. I had started to thaw next to a cozy fireplace and the first sip of Cognac brought me back to almost normal. I took off my jacket and within minutes the aroma of a delicious dinner filled my nostrils. I had not had a regular home cooked meal in days. Herb potatoes, chicken in a thick mushroom sauce and fresh asparagus tasted incredible! After some small conversation, I thanked them profoundly for their hospitality and passed out in the couch closest to the dying embers in the fireplace. I felt his wife covering me with a blanket and went into dream world.

I still remember the dreams from that night, Asu and I had gotten married and moved to the Florida Keys where I was a part-time family doctor and had a dog named "surf" who was the best Frisbee catcher in the Keys. Asu and I were at a Dolphin game where I was trying to explain to her why the "two minute warning" lasted over 5 minutes.

When I finally woke up the next day, I did not know what planet had Scotty beamed me up to (I am such a "Trekkie"). The day looked beautiful outside, it was all white and the sun was shining, my Timex watch told me it was 12.36 PM! Jackes said we could tow my car back to the main road with his truck but we had to have lunch first. This time I offered to cook for them. Yes my friends, I have not forgotten this is still a cookbook. I looked around the kitchen and came up with a "brunch" idea. Here you go:

20- *SURVIVAL TORTILLA (Survival Omelet)*

• 3 large potatoes or 4 if you want. Peeled and sliced thin, not lengthwise but circumference like, get it?

• A bunch of eggs, maybe 8 or so, beaten but not defeated.

• Half a pound of cubed cooking ham

• One large onion diced small

• A handful of Parsley

• Small can of sweet peas

• Salt and pepper

• Olive oil.

In a large deep skillet about 2 or 3 inches deep, pour olive oil until it covers the bottom don't make it into an olive oil "pool", just enough to cover the bottom of the skillet. On MEDIUM-LOW heat start to cook the potatoes, don't let them stick. Once they become fairly soft (test with fork), take them out with a strainer ladle and place inside the beaten eggs. Add salt, pepper, parsley and sweet peas to the mix as well. Clean the skillet of any potato residue that may have stuck to the bottom, re-oil a little bit, turn stove on low and briefly sauté the onions and the ham. About five minutes. When this is done, add to the mix of eggs and potatoes that should have already contain the parsley, salt pepper etc. Pour the whole mix in the skillet. The left over oil from the ham and onions should be ok, if you need to add a little more, go ahead, make my day. Cook on low until the edges begin to appear cooked. Run a plastic spatula around the edges to loosen the omelet from the pan. Shake the skillet a few times in order to keep the mix from sticking to the bottom, here comes the tricky part, if you have a high degree of confidence, flip the omelet over like the professional chefs on TV, do it over the sink just in case, NO FEAR here, if you think the omelets will end on the floor or the ceiling by doing this, a safer thing is to turn on the broiler and place the skillet a couple of inches under it, this will finish cooking the top of the omelet and give it a nice gold color, WATCH it, don't burn it! Carefully you can slide the omelet into a large flat dish. The depth of the omelet of course depends on the depth of the skillet; in Spain you see them around 3 inches thick. The ingredients can be modified, get creative, almost anything goes with eggs, sweet red peppers, mushrooms (need to cook them first), asparagus, and so on. Cut it like a pie, have a piece of French bread, we did that morning.

The coffee was nice and strong, I felt like a brand new man. I gave his wife a big hug and Jackes drove me to the car. Ironically it could be seen from the road, the night, snow and my mental state of tiredness probably played tricks on me. It was not difficult to toe the small Fiat. I thanked Jackes and promised I would write.

He waited to make sure I could start the car and after the third try, the engine came to life, I headed back to Spain, the town of San Sebastian on the Northern coast was my destination. I had heard about an international film festival being held there and it seemed like the right place to go. My spirits were up; I filed the previous night experience under "fate and survival" and hit the road.

Driving through the Northern coast of Spain is an absolutely beautiful experience. You can watch the rough seas breaking on high rock cliffs. The Basque area of Spain is reminiscent of the Vikings (the real ones) and their local language has no known roots. The architecture, typical folk dresses and dances remind you of Viking culture. San Sebastian claims to be one of the best planned cities in Europe. It has very clean streets and the best seafood anywhere. I was getting excited and upon my arrival I decided to stay at a "hostal" (a small family owned hotel) in the old section of town. Having to decide between food and sleep, logic dictated sleep would come first. I checked in and not bothering to shower hit the sack and fell into a dreamless sleep. Five o'clock PM was the magic hour to wake up. I was hungry and thirsty but decided to shower away the smells of the road. The weather was cool but not too bad outside so I put on a pair of Levy's, my black light turtleneck sweater and loafers, splashed some Paco Rabanne on my face and headed out ready to eat the whole town! Not far from the hostal I found a tavern right by the water that seemed to have a lively crowd and a detectable delicious food smell. I found a place to seat at the counter, noticing the lack of curiosity from the crowd as opposed to Andalusia. Northern Basque Spaniards are taller than most other regions and have for the most part light complexions. I noticed many were speaking mostly in Basque. Basque was used by intelligence operatives during WWII to keep the Germans from detection of codes. I spoke Spanish fluently but would make it a point to learn some Basque expressions soon.

I asked the man behind the bar what he recommended to eat and before he answered, as if by magic, a mug filled with a thick white wine was brought in front of me. Now I did see a few people staring a little, I'm sure to gauge my reaction after tasting this wine. I sensed this as sort of a "test", a ritual of passage or acceptance. I lifted the mug, downed the whole thing in one hit and asked for a refill. I saw a few smiles and heard some comments in Basque that seemed to be favorably directed at me. I had never tasted this wine, it was thick and very strong, not fruity with a nutty flavor, I really liked it. I had made a good start in this new town. A plate was placed in front of me that contained smoked sardines that were bigger than Jaws, marinated artichokes hearts and a few slices of the local cured ham (Prosciuto style) served with magnificent bread. I devoured the whole thing in record time. The artichokes marinade tasted like anchovies and olives. I tell you it was so good! The crowd around me seemed a little surprised when I ordered another serving and more "mug wine". Before I knew it, I had made some conversation and they were teaching me the basic Basque phrases and all seemed very pleased at my willingness to learn. I made them laugh with my story about getting stuck in the snow two days before. The mug wine kept on flowing and it was really warming me up, and at one point between sips, I noticed a face in the crowd that seemed to show a different interest level, another moment in time, new territory to be explored, a new fork on the road, another incursion into the twilight zone. She was blonde, tall and pretty. I decided to do an exploration tour and see what possibilities were there. Her name was Nuntxi, it was a Basque name, and phonetically it was pronounced "Noontzy". She was friendly, we stood closer to each other and the rest of her friends seemed to get the hint and started to slowly move away leaving us alone. Numtxi laughed when I told her my friends in Seville called me "Vikingo" (Viking). We hit it off very well, talked about medical school, the differences in culture between Seville and Northern Spain, I spoke about Miami, South Beach and the Dolphins, she had never seen American football. As you probably know, Soccer rules in Spain, they call it "futbol". I hate the stupid sport (sorry Soccer moms), there is nothing like the smell of a hot dog, the sound of a marching band, the cheer of the crowd at a Dolphins, or a Canes game (University of Miami).

The night started to welcome its wee hours and about 2 or 3 in the morning and having consumed a large number of mug wine I felt an altered state of mind where time and space had no meaning. I have a great resistance to wine, but this one was different and much more powerful than the typical red wine I was used to drinking.

My first recollection after that night was waking up in my hostal room to a knock on the door that sounded like if Godzilla was mad and wanted to eat me. I managed to get up and move toward the general direction of the sound, which would be the front door. Opening the door a few inches I attempted the difficult task of "speech" which was made almost impossible by the Velcro lock between my tongue and the roof of my mouth. Finally I managed to focus my eyes and mumble some sound that was answered by a gentle female voice who said: Hi, this is Nuntxi, I just came to see if you were all right". I managed another complicated task, opening the door wider and waving my hand for her to come in. I remembered a scene from the movie "The Sting" where Robert Redford finds himself in a similar situation and buries his head in a sink full of ice. I then heard Spock's voice saying: "Ice IS the logical thing". I asked Nuntxi if she could get me some, she happily agreed and as she left the room, I somehow managed to put my pants on. The ice age came and my head found it, feeling started to return, a couple of brain cells waived at each other. I asked Nuntxi about the night before and she said that at one point I was singing some Dolphin song (The Miami Dolphins fight song I figured) and that I had mentioned somebody named "Asu". She had brought me back to the hostal and had tucked me in. Nuntxi smiled, said not to worry and asked if I felt like lunch.

After a shower (she did really wait downstairs, really), we went out to a nice tavern where we had several cheeses, some of that delicious ham, fresh tomatoes, artichokes and I did have one of the local beers called Keller 18, a brewery owned by a German brew master who had married a local woman and decided to stay in San Sebastian.

Nuntxi and I walked around the peers and other parts of the city. The film festival was in full swing and we made it to a couple of shows. At one time we saw the actor Peter Sellers and I got his autograph for her. Yes, a recipe is coming here.

Later that afternoon we ran into some of her friends that were present the night before and she was invited to bring her American friend to a Christmas party at one of the houses. I thought that was awful nice of them to invite me. In a show of appreciation for this hospitality, an idea started to brew in my mind. I would cook something they had not seen before and bring it to the party that night. What would that dish be? Get ready for:

21-MACHO CHILI

- Half pound of ground beef, half pound of ground pork.

- One pound of chili beans or small red beans.

- One large diced onion

- 21 garlic cloves, ok ok, maybe 15, chopped small

- Two large tomatoes cut in cubes

- One 8 oz can of tomato sauce

- A bunch of parsley and cilantro, chopped

- One large green pepper chopped small

- One spoonful of cumin powder

- Salt and pepper, to your taste

- 1/4 cup of paprika

- Hot peppers. (Jalapenos, Habaneros, Poblanos, whatever you can find is ok, just make sure you know how hot you want the chili, don't ruin it by having it burn a whole in your mouth. Unless you are from one of the states near the Mexican border. Habaneros are one of the hottest peppers. Just choose wisely. Use maybe two or three, chopped small.

Nuntxi and I spent the rest of the afternoon shopping for the ingredients and had a lot of fun, we had to substitute a few things, Cilantro was impossible to find so we used more parsley. At the end, we came close to producing a decent chili. We got to her friend's house early and after proper introductions to her parents I started to become familiar with the kitchen. The weather had turned much colder, perfect for chili! As I started to sort and prepare the ingredients a Keller 18 was placed in my hand, I really liked that beer and made a mental note to take some back to Seville. After a while, more people began to arrive and of course they all converged in the kitchen and had a bunch of questions on everything from American politics and lifestyles to medical school.

Here is how this dish was prepared:

Throw the beans in a large heavy pot (here we go with the word "throw" again, must be a macho thing) Two to one water-bean ratio. Add a little salt and cook forever on low heat. Pot should be covered. It should take a good 3 hours or more. You want the beans to be creamy and cooked all the way.

In a skillet, pour some olive oil and make what is called a "sofrito" by cooking the all the ingredients together except the meat and beans. Cook for about 5 minutes and then throw the meat until is browned and mix the whole thing well with a wooden spoon, of course on medium heat. Dump all the water from the already cooked beans and throw the skillet contents with the beans. Cover pot. The secret to good chili is to cook it long and slow. Since the beans were already cooked, I just turned the stove on simmer, had another Keller 18 and started to mingle with the crowd. By now the night had arrived, there were many other dishes at the party, the Basque love to eat and eat well.

I was very pleased to see the chili pot almost empty by midnight; it went very well with further consumption of Keller 18. The Basque can also drink as I quickly had learned. I noticed several guests were drinking the mug wine that had played havoc with my brain on my first night, and decided to stay away from it and drink the semi-dark brew called Keller 18. I had squeezed a few in the freezer; ice cold beer was a strange concept in most of Spain.

Everyone thanked me for introducing chili to them; I had made friends during my short stay in San Sebastian. The crowd started to thin and since the weather had gotten windy and cold, Nuntxi offered to drive me back to the Hostal. She had done all the driving so I had left my Fiat at the Hostal. Nuntxi drove a Seat 600, the Spanish version of the Seat. The car looked like an egg but was very efficient. The Hostal was next to an ocean inlet bordered by a sea wall over 15 feet tall. We noticed the waves were hitting the wall with such force that it reached the street. We got out of the car and faced the wind and the cold to watch the waves. It was a tremendous experience, the sound of the crashing waves foaming at the top, the anticipation of the next wave, the game of daring to get close to the sea wall and avoid getting sprayed by the water. At one point we cuddled for warmth and our cold lips found each other with a slight salty taste from the sea water. I then decided to spend the rest of my Christmas holiday in San Sebastian...

The next morning I was happy to see sunlight through my window, the wind was still blowing hard and the waves had not ceased to pound the sea wall. I had some coffee and buttered bread at the Hostal and bought a copy of The Herald Tribune for the only purpose of finding out if the Dolphins had made the playoffs. Reading some news from home, a taste of homesickness filled my heart. One thing was for sure, no matter how much fun all the travels can bring, there's just no place like home for Christmas. I always had to maintain that "home-link" in order to keep my sanity. This was all magnified at Christmas time as you think of the lights, chestnuts roasting, Bing Crosby's "Silent Night", and all the things that make us want to be in America. As I was lost in thought sipping a second cup of coffee, humidity blurred my vision. I tried to snap out of it and make the best out of my time in San Sebastian.

After about three days of exploring the city and enjoying the film festival I got to meet Nuntxi's parents. They had already heard about me from some of the other parents. The meeting went well, they were nice and friendly. Later that day an invitation was extended by her parents to visit their real house, a stone 18th century house in the nearby province of Soria. This sounded a little exciting; the house was located smack in the middle of wheat fields belonging to her parents. I followed them in my car on the main road that lead to a secondary road and eventually it lead to some non traveled dirt road that almost made it impossible for the Fiat to maneuver. There was an absence of electricity, TV, telephones. There was what seemed to be total silence. It was a very peaceful feeling. The house was very cold inside, it felt like walking inside a refrigerator. There was not even a radio! I helped (with great enthusiasm) Nuntxi's father feed some logs to the stone fireplace, a dark wood I did not recognize. Then, what does a South Beach bum know about firewood? The fire came alive after a couple of tries and I stayed close to it so my fingers could start the thawing process. Nuntxi poured us a glass of thick homemade wine that tasted of clove and cinnamon spices. It was really delicious. We went out for a walk and looking at the wheat fields, the words from our national anthem "for amber waves of grain" took on a whole new meaning. I had never seen wheat fields before. The days at San Sebastian and now in Soria became very easy and free of responsibilities, no schedules, no exams but there was always that strange feeling of homesickness, not just for the USA, but for the warmer climate in Seville, I thought of Asu and her parents, for the rest of the gang, my buddies. I was hoping they missed the Viking as well. This felt like being in a strange planet in a quadrant thousands of light years away from the Federation (For those in West Palm, Rio Linda and the left coast in general, that was Star Trek lingo, meaning I felt very, very far from my home turf).

Before nighttime, her parents cooked (on a wooden stove using that same dark wood) some very tender steaks, garlic potatoes and sweet roasted peppers that were the best I ever had. I may include that recipe in "Memories and Spice II" I had some more of that home made red wine (warm this time) and it really felt good going down. Night had fallen and we were using candles. The stars were breathtaking, with no lights around; they were clearly seen by the billions. I saw at least five falling stars and did make some wishes. It was Christmas Eve and suddenly I felt very tired. I heard Bing Crosby in the back of my mind singing Silent Night followed by Jose Feliciano's Feliz Navidad, all in my mind of course. It was bed time, Nuntxi walked me to my room where a brass bed looked frozen, I turned on a catalytic gas heater pointing at the bed, kept my clothes on except the shoes and went to sleep in total absolute silence. It was 7.00 PM.

Dec 25th. Soria province, Spain, 9.30 AM Total silence was broken by distant voices, I struggled for recall of time and place. It was cold in my room that Christmas morning, the sun came through my blinds and the smell of country bacon and burning wood filled my senses. I almost thought about looking for gifts under my bed (that had been oh so long ago...). There was no Christmas tree, no jingles. I went down stairs and wished everyone a Merry Christmas in Basque (I had learned a few key phrases by now). They all laughed and said it was pronounced very well.

After eating a hearty breakfast Nuntxi took me for a walk around the edges of the closest wheat field and we spoke of how nice our meeting had been since my arrival at San Sebastian and about the possibility of continuing this encounter with a visit to Seville. Nuntxi said I should not feel obligated in any way and I was welcome to stay with them as long as I could. She understood if I wanted to leave. It was time for the Viking to hit the road, this was not my territory. They all understood. Later that day I packed and accepted some home made chorizos (Spanish sausage) and some of that red wine. There was enough gas in the Fiat to make it to the next town. God byes, kisses, a good hug and an open invitation to come back were left behind as I hit the road old Jack and headed SOUTH!

More cooking next.

22- ROPA VIEJA (Cuban Shredded Beef)

This is one of my favorite Cuban dishes. I have never been able to get it totally right but I'm close. This dish is called Ropa Vieja which translated means "Old Clothes", hence the "shredded" status. No story here, just food ok? But actually there was this Irish girl that... No really, just kidding! Here is what you need to get:

- Two pounds of flank steak
- One large green pepper sliced thin length wise
- One large onion chopped medium.
- 4 garlic cloves chopped small
- Salt and Pepper, about a teaspoon each
- 10 Manzanilla olives
- 1/2 cup of white vinegar
- One teaspoon of cumin powder
- 8 oz dry white wine. (or dry sherry)
- Small can of tomato paste
- 8 oz can of tomato sauce

Cook the flank, if using a pressure cooker, it'll be faster (about 25minutes), if using a regular pot, cook for about 2 1/2 hours. Make sure you have enough water to cover the meat in either a pressure cooker or a regular pot. Of course, do cover either of them. If you have never used a pressure cooker before, learn how to use it! Please! It can be dangerous if not used properly. Salt the water or add a chicken or beef bouillon.

Once the meat is cooked, it should be more than fork tender, place it in a large tray, when it cools a little, shred it with a fork, in small shreds ok, as small as you can, not microscopic but small. In a large skillet about one inch deep sauté onions, peppers and garlic using olive oil on medium heat (about 5 minutes) Olive oil should always be used on medium heat because of its low boiling point. Add the rest of the ingredients and mix well, stir once in a while. Don't forget, the beef is already cooked so don't overkill. Some people like a dash of hot sauce, that's ok but again, this is a Cuban dish, not Mexican, Cuban cuisine does not kill food with burning hot sauce. Serve with maduros and white rice, a cold beer would be just fine here. Oh this is so good, it's making me hungry!

The school year went faster than anticipated and in the summer of 79 with a lot of help from my friends I was facing my last year in Spain. This had brought a bitter sweet feeling since there were so many great memories and yet, it was time to finish this rotation, all different aspects of life are to be considered like medical rotations according to my "Bro" Dr. Alan Peterson whom I met after medical school at Memorial Hospital where we ran a regular MASH unit. But that "rotation" deserves a whole book in itself. Perhaps we will write a co-authored book someday (come to think of it, that would be dangerous)

Back in Seville everything seemed to have a different flavor knowing this was to be my last year. I had gotten to know the culture in Southern Spain as good as the locals thanks to Asu and her family. A very special relationship had formed; it wasn't just Asu, but her family that had become sort of my family in Spain. That was also a subject that occupied my mind that year as I often rehearsed in my mind what the "good byes" would be like. I saw Alicia several times in between her flights and we did go back to Rafaelo's a couple of times. Eva kept my mailbox filled with letters and perfume, she would often send things from London. Asu, well, she was just there, her parents and relatives had taken for granted that the two of us would end up together somehow. I knew deep down that my life belonged in the US; I could not stay in Spain. It was hard to keep the proper mental perspective that year. My songwriting was prolific during that period and I started to perform on a regular basis at a real cool place called "The Hollywood Pub", an American style pub which hosted a live radio show to most of Southern Spain. It was like a piece of the USA, many American students frequented this pub and I began to draw a bit of a fan club who wanted to hear American-Folk-Country-blues gender music. My Martin D-12-20 was getting some workout (my guitar for those in the left coast). After my gig, we would often end up at another place owned by a retired American Air Force officer who was stationed in Spain and had married a beautiful Spanish woman. His place was called "Sloppy Joes" and one could eat a good American style hamburger there. I knew Guy and his wife very well. One night after a gig I ran into an American called John Dupree who asked me if I could use a banjo player. He had been at the pub and said he could play many of the songs I did. I agreed and the next night John showed up with a bunch of friends and we went at it. He was really good and could change chords on a fly, had a sense of what I was going to do with a song which was not always easy since I did a lot of improvisation (Rich Ventura is laughing right now). This brought a lot of memories from my days stationed at Ft. Polk, Louisiana (Home of the Infantry soldier) and "The Folk Machine" days with Rich Ventura, Cindy Ventura and Marty Benjamin. Richard played left handed guitar and sometimes a "washtub" base (Hillbilly instrument made of a real tin washtub, string and a broomstick). Then we were influenced by bluegrass music a lot and we played stuff like "12 Bar Blues" and "Foggy Mountain Breakdown" This provided a great background for that night in Seville when John played his banjo. He was surprised I knew all those songs. I have to say, the South ROSE again that night! As the music flowed like a mountain stream. We knocked their socks off!!

There were some exchange students from Virginia and South Carolina who got "down" that night, beer flowed, and I even saw a student holding a can of Budweiser, probably obtained from a serviceman stationed with the U.S. Navy at the nearby ROTA base. We played until we ran out of material. The radio broadcast was only one hour but we kept on playing. Suddenly the whole crowd started a rendition of God Bless America, we followed and played along. The few Spaniards left in the pub did not know what to make of this. We were taking over!

Around what I perceived to be three in the morning, fingers almost bleeding from playing, we decided food was called for (yep, here it comes). It had been an unforgettable night I will not forget. John invited a bunch of us to a kind of college dorm where he was staying. I put the guitar away and followed them in the Fiat, top down of course, wind upon my face (God, it sounds like some Paul Simon song. Not that that is bad, it just reminded me of one of his songs). John cooked that night, food, not breakfast, regular diner food, yes, it was around 4:00 AM!

23- DUPREE'S SEAFOOD AND CHICKEN

- 4 green onions sliced thin
- One small jalapeno pepper minced
- 1 large carrot sliced in small sections about 1/2 inch.
- 3 minced garlic cloves
- 1/2 pound of fresh okra, yeah Okra, don't be afraid.
- One cup of can corn (DelMonte's fresh harvest is good)
- I cup of snow peas (before the snow melts)
- One cup of parsley, chopped (don't forget to rinse it before use)
- 1 teaspoon of white pepper
- 12 large shrimps peeled and deveined
- 1.2 cup of heavy cream
- 3boneless chicken breasts cut in one inch strips
- White dry wine, about a bottle, 8 oz for the dish and the rest for you
- Salt to taste

In a large heavy pot pour olive oil until the bottom has a thin cover. Turn stove on medium. Salt and pepper the chicken strips with your hands and place inside (where else would you place them?), Wash hands afterwards of course. When the chicken strips look somewhat cooked but not brown, add the rest of the ingredients except the shrimp. Mix well and cook for about 15 minutes with a cover lid. Always add shrimp or other seafood last since cooking time is a lot shorter and you don't want to overcook it. Open the pot (so you can put the shrimp inside) and place shrimp in, mix again and turn stove on low. Cook for another 6 minutes or so. The okra will give this dish sort of a stew texture. What, you don't like Okra? Skip it them, no problem, it won't be as good though.

John took some beer out of the fridge, Curzcampo, a local brand hat lacked kick but it did the job that night. I had two bowls with a hunk of day old bread that was still ok. John and I became good friends and kept on playing music together at the Hollywood Pub. Playing for live radio was a first to us; especially for an hour show you need a lot of material. We managed between my original songs and his bluegrass stuff. The gig had grown in fan numbers and we were bringing in a faithful following. Word began to spread and recognition started to grow. A few articles were published in the local newspapers about the big American and his banjo player who provided great blues and bluegrass. My grades started to drop, music was taking over. This was a great rush, one incredible "rotation" as Bro Peterson likes to say. The show's producer would invite us often for dinner and music events. During one such event, a concert by a nationally known singer, the show's producer (I swear I can't remember his name) introduced me to the singer after the concert. I liked his music, hid did a lot of original stuff and his lyrics had depth. He showed some admiration for our music and asked about my inspiration for the original songs, to which I responded: The pursuit of women and all its consequences" which made him laugh and he agreed that to be his inspiration as well. His name was Peralez.

One of the greatest thrills of any performer is recognition by a total stranger. This happened on an occasion when we were trying every kind of Solera sherry at a local wine maker out of the typical tourist routes when the owner of the establishment was speaking to some other local folk and referred to me as: "El cantao (pronunciation strength on the "o") del Pub Americano que a mi hija le guhta oi" Translation: This is that singer from the American Pub my daughter likes so much! My friends, that just made my day. The statement was followed by several handshakes and an offer to try more sherry. By the way, this place had its own aged barrels in the back and specialized in Solera, Fino, Manzanilla. These are dry to medium dry Sherries, properly consumed in small glasses and accompanied by big pimento stuffed olives, hard Manchego cheese, cured ham and stuffed artichoke hearts. We spent a good 6 hours at the place. Feeling the effects of the wine, I told the owner it would be my privilege to invite him and his family (daughter included of course) to the Pub for our next show that Friday night and I would mention his winery on the radio. He fully agreed and thanked me. To the best of my recollection, my roommate Pablo drove me home that night. I knew I had found a new friend in Sevilla and had a strong feeling his daughter would be at the Pub that Friday due to my extensive medical training and instincts that had never guided me wrong when it came to wine, women and music.

Friday did arrive, Showtime! John started to tune that banjo, I had a brand new set of Martin strings on my guitar (my last set I had brought from the states). I noticed the usual crowd beginning to arrive, mostly American exchange students and some personnel from the American Consulate with their wives along with several locals who were curious or dug the mountain music and the American scene. Just before the lights dimmed and watching the countdown often done on a live radio show, the owner of the winery arrived with several people, his wife, some friends and a very attractive girl, maybe 20 or 21 years old. Luckily I had reserved a front table, they sat down and I caught a very friendly, endangering sweet smile from this girl. Obviously Antonio's daughter. The lights were dimmed and we had a sign from the DJ that we had 10 seconds to the red light which indicated we were LIVE. If any of you reading this book has ever performed, there is no need to explain what that moment feels like; the rush is like nothing else. We hit it with "Foggy Mountain Breakdown", one of our standard songs; John's banjo I swear was producing smoke in the middle of the song. It was the best rendition we had ever done. John was incredible! The crowd started to clap strongly after the strong finish, my eyes drifted toward Antonio's table and caught his daughter clapping her heart out with a look that said "I'm your biggest fan and you can do no wrong!" Ahh, life should always be like that. I introduced her and his family to the audience, mentioned her father's fine wines along with the fine character in him and his family. The girl was speechless as she brought her hands to her eyes. It was a rare beautiful moment to be remembered in this book, shared with you and cherished in my mind forever.

I know some of you may be asking yourselves: Did this guy ever finish medical school?? Yes he did! By bringing the term "cramming" to new heights.

We finished the show that night in great fashion with "Rocky Town Tennessee" Antonio's daughter Concepcion (which translated means "conception", hopefully not an omen) brought us some flowers and kissed us in the cheek (good start). This was one of the sweetest moments I ever had on stage. As Conce (short for Concepcion) kept on thanking me and being excited I noticed a guy at her table with sort of an inquisitive look so in the interest of US-Spain relations, I walked over and in friendly version of the local dialect introduced myself. He quickly smiled and said he had never listened to that music gender before. Like my mom always told me, "son, you should have been a diplomat or a lawyer". The guy happened to be Conce's brother and I made him feel at ease in the normal protection of his little sister.

Antonio extended an open invitation to his place and before leaving, gave Conce and me a moment alone. Whatever could have happened between Conce and I was decided by the fates as Asu (remember her?) was a regular at the Pub (not there that night) and that would have created an uneasy situation. Our relationship was somewhat strange, we had never made formal commitments, yet, and I felt some obligation to her and her family. Don't ask me to explain. Female readers probably understood my situation perfectly!

The following week provided to be a challenge at the pub, Asu was there as usual. As John and I were getting ready to start playing, I noticed a group coming in headed by... yep; you guessed it, Antonio and his family, Conce included. Somehow, Asu gave her one of those looks that only women can give and relay a meaningful message that said: "Don't fool with him". This look went seemingly unnoticed as Conce walked all the way to the stage and gave me a kiss on the cheek. John looked at me with a worried look and whispered away from his mike (boy you are in deep s———). We started to play and all troubles seemed to disappear. At the end it was ok for some reason. Conce asked me if I knew something in Spanish, coincidentally, I had been working on a song using a poem from Antonio Machado, a very famous poet in Andalusia that I liked very much. I said sure, and John looked at me saying "go for it, I'll try to follow" The subject of the poem was about a journey being far better than the arrival at its destination. The song was a ballad, the lights were dimmed even further and John picked the banjo in a beautiful way. I put everything I had into the song and dedicated it to Conce AND Asu. No fear dude! When the song ended, the remaining locals were the ones standing and clapping from their hearts. The song seemed to have a soothing effect over the possibly difficult situation. As John and I were putting our instruments away, I saw Asu and Conce actually talking to each other. I stayed away; I knew the boundaries and rules were being discussed. I never found out what was said at that conversation, but things were smooth from that point on.

Word got out about my song from the adaptation of Machado's poem and calls came in the radio the next day. People wondering about who was this American that normally plays blues and mountain music and had written a song based on Machado's famous poem sung in perfect Spanish. This thing grew thanks to the interest of the show's producer and the suggestion from Jose Luis Perales, the one singer I had met who suggested this could be taken to a much higher level. Life seemed to have taken a new turn for me; the scary part was that I liked it. Deep down I always knew I belonged on the stage. There was even some talk about going into a national TV show and some studio recording., more shows, travel etc. This would mean full time music during my last year of medical school. Some decisions had to be made.

Those decisions would be made over food of course (you forgot this was a cook book ha?). All those who were close to me gathered at my apartment, Asu, Pablo (El Gallo), Jose, John (the banjo man), Conce, yes she was there also. This was not going to be easy, I had come here to study medicine, I was close to finishing, and show business was a totally different direction. Jose Sabates and Pablo (my two closest friends) wanted me to go all the way into the music; Jose actually offered to be my manager. We would eat first and then decide. It was time for:

24- DECISION CHICKEN

- One cup of honey
- 1/2 cup of lemon juice
- A handful of rosemary leaves
- One tablespoon of crushed red pepper
- 3 lbs of chicken breasts
- Salt and pepper

Combine all the ingredients in a bowl, mix well. Rub the breasts (the chicken breasts). Let them rest for an hour. In a large skillet, pour some oil, not olive this time, corn, peanut etc. On medium heat, cook chicken on both sides for about ten minutes depending on the thickness of the breasts. Serve with white rice and something green, a plate or a napkin, seriously, maybe some broccoli or sweet peas.

We ate and drank San Miguel beer, a cut above Cruzcampo brand. When finished, I took my bottle of Cardenal Mendoza brandy, prepared the right glasses by heating them and we all had a toast for "The Viking" (incredible how the name had stuck) and his future whatever it might be. With the help and good sense of Asu and Conce, a compromised was later reached. I would still play at the pub on Fridays but no more than that. I would finish my last year in Spain.

Many thoughts played and bounced off the windmills of my mind that year. The future, what it would be like to leave all the relationships I had made over the last few years, the end of "easy street" as further internship training in the US was fast approaching. There were many advantages in this way of life I had credit at every bar and restaurant of importance in Seville and some in other cities as well. Rents are low, palm trees grow but I keep on thinking about, making my way back. Ok, those are words from a Neil Diamond song, but it was the way I felt.

The year went faster than anticipated and before I knew it winter came to Sevilla with miserable gray, wet and windy cold. I was not going to be able to go home this Christmas due to late exams and hospital rotations, not a good prospect for the Viking.

The last day of class before the break had been a long tiring day, my spirits had dropped in unison with the lousy weather. I started to drive back to the apartment as a cold drizzle began to fall. The Fiat turned into a road leaving the school and I my face felt a cold drop of rain leaking through the now worn out top. I don't quite recall all my thoughts going home that day and maybe they are not worth remembering. As I finally pulled in front of the apartment, I noticed a raincoat clad figure emerging from a taxi. I stayed in my car waiting for the image to become clearer as the driver helped her get the luggage out of the trunk. When recognition crossed my brain synapses, a ray

of sunshine illuminated my face as Eve stared at me and said "Are you going to help with my luggage?" There IS a
GOD! I jumped out of my car in one swift move into the now heavier rain and met her with a kiss. Her first question
was""Are you mad I did not warn you about my visit?" I replied: "What took you so long?" We both laughed and got
out of the rain.

I decided to take Eve to Rafaelo's that night and spend some time alone with her. Over dinner she explained of her
wish to see me knowing this was my last year in Spain. Of course she mentioned some issues that had to be settled in
her mind about any possible future between us. We had kept good correspondence since we had met and many key
words were written on fancy perfumed letters. She was also completing medical school in England and some decisions
had to be made. Some things were settled that night and a final understanding was reached that her life was in
England and mine would be in the states. Once this was cleared, it made things easier. The following night I decided
to invite the few friends that were left in Sevilla that year as many had already finished school and were gone. (No,
no Asu or Conce this time, I may be crazy but not that crazy). I cooked something different that night inspired by the
cold weather. It's time for:

25- GREAT BALLS OF FIRE!

- One pound of lean ground beef

- Handful of chopped parsley

- One egg, beaten (but not defeated)

- Salt and pepper, about a teaspoon of each

- Bread crumbs (Progresso is great)

- One or two hot chilly peppers, Habaneros are very hot, Jalapenos are better. Depends on how
  much fire you need.

- Fresh Ginger, about a teaspoon, grated. (Ginger powder ok, not great, but ok)

Easy thing. Mix all ingredients in a large bowl, mix them well. Using your hands here is great fun and
it also serves as therapy, remember when we were kids how we liked to play with silly putty or mud
in my case? It made us feel good! So, when the mix is all mixed, make some balls, small, medium or
large, it doesn't matter. If you wet your hands a little, it becomes easier. At this point you can bake
them in the oven using a baking tray painted with butter or you can use one of those baking paper
sheets. Bake at 350 degrees for 30 to 45 minutes depending on how hot the oven is. The balls should
be brown and crispy outside. Serve them in a pretty tray on a bed of lettuce with those fancy tooth

picks. I'm sure my female readers know what I mean. Garnish with slices of limes, squeeze a couple on the balls if you like.

We had other snack foods that night, chorizo (Spanish cured sausage), shrimp, and fresh breads and drank some of Antonio's finest Sherries which I had saved. We sang Christmas carols and got a little homesick. Eve liked the group very much and told us about traditional Christmas songs and foods in England. The following day the weather turned sunny but still very cold as we rode into town so Eva could see some of the typical tourist sites. She thought I was crazy riding with the top down. The Fiat had a good heating system and it was fun to feel the cold wind on our faces. We did some shopping (women's eternal and universal need). I had a peaceful easy feeling (line from an Eagles song). Eve told me her father had approved her trip to Spain since the "lad" (me) had made a jolly good impression on him. That night I wanted to cook something special for her so after all the touristing and shopping I went to "El Corte Ingles", a version of COSTCO where great meats in special cuts could be obtained. I asked the butcher to get me the best "eye of the round" he could find. My mother's favorite dish was Cuban style pot roast and I wanted to cook that for Eve. Don't read anything into this ok; I was just trying to be nice. In memory of my mother I'll call this dish:

26- DELIA'S BOLICHE

- One lean eye of the round. Around 3 pounds.
- 4 bay leaves
- Salt and pepper
- One cup of sweet peas
- Red wine, a Cabernet would be fine.
- One thin chorizo, (Spanish Sausage), this can be substituted for a medium pealed carrot.

Here we go, there will be some initial work involved here so pay attention. You will stuff the eye of the round with the chorizo or carrot. The way to do this is by holding the meat firmly with a clean towel on the cutting board (wood preferred) and with a long knife make an incision through the middle of the meat, length wise deep enough to stuff the chorizo or the carrot. Be careful here; don't loose any fingers over this. If you are not good with knives, have the butcher do it for you. Explain your purpose to the man, be nice about it. Once this is done the rest is easy. Rub the meat with salt and pepper, do it abundantly. In a large heavy pot pour about an inch of water and some of the red wine along with the bay leaves. Turn stove on medium low and place the meat in it. Cover the pot. This will be a long cooking dish so just relax, allow plenty of time, have a drink or two but do check the pot every 10 minutes or so and when you do, turn the meat making sure there is enough water. You don't want to cover the meat with water, only about an inch or so. Pour more wine as well. Keep on turning the meat every 10 or 15 minutes. Cook for at least 2 to 2 1/2 hours. Take it our and let it rest for 10 minutes. This is important. Slice the whole thing in 1/2 inch slices. If you like them thinner that's ok but half inch works great. The meat should be totally tender, fork tender. Place slices in a large serving tray. The center showing the carrot or chorizo gives it a neat appearance. Pour the juice from the pot over the meat. The green sweet peas will look nice. Avoid the bay leaves. Serve with white rice and maduros.

Eve read a book while I was doing my kitchen chores, I was thankful she was there. The weather turned colder and windy, thoughts about our future began to creep in the windmills of my mind. I sipped from a bottle of San Miguel beer as I was telling Eve about my gig at the pub and all that had happened, the chance to go on TV, the decision to just do one night at the pub and finish school. She listened and told me I was some kind of free soul and that the music will always stay with me. There was a warm feeling here that in a strong way, it all seemed right and yet.......

My thoughts were interrupted by Eve asking when dinner would be ready. I sliced the meat, cooked white rice (no maduros in Spain) and served some white asparagus tips with a vinaigrette sauce. We ate in a somewhat peaceful silent way, had a couple of glasses of Paternina Rioja and felt mellow and cozy. We sat in the couch with the lights turned low and Eve leaned on my chest, she asked me what I missed most from home and I told her it was the small mundane things that got to you and made you homesick. The Dolphins, South Beach sand football, my friends, the late night show with Johnny Carson, the smell of summer rain in South Florida, Christmas Carols etc. She also said some things along the same lines about London and a tiny voice kept on whispering in my ear, it was time for the Viking to go on home. It was difficult to sleep that night as I noticed her eyes were also opened. The next morning I started playing some old Christmas albums with Bing Crosby Stills and Nash, just playing with your mind, it was Bing Crosby. Eve woke up to the smell of coffee and came out of the bedroom with a small box in her hand, a gift from London, a crystal dolphin! I had also gotten her a gift while we were shopping, an old antique jewelry box made of rare woods. We were both surprised and accepted each other's hugs and kisses. We had coffee and decided to go into town to shop for a Christmas dinner. I always yearn for the typical Cuban Christmas Eve dinner consisting of roasted pork, black beans, white rice, maduros and "yucca" (also known as Cassava), however these items were hard to find so I improvised with something totally new. CHRISTMAS SALMON INSTEAD

27- CHRISTMAS SALMON INSTEAD

- One large salmon fillet enough for two hungry people
- One cup of dry dill
- 1/2 cup of Rosemary
- One handful of parsley or cilantro.
- Lime juice
- Salt and pepper
- Spanish Paprika
- Mayonnaise

Salt and pepper the salmon fillet. Bake at 350 degrees for 30 minutes. (I really don't know how to make the sign for the word "degree" since the "o" seems too big and the 0 is even bigger. OK, so, Ah ain't Bill Gates) While the fish is baking add all the other ingredients in a blender. About 3 spoonfuls of mayo, the juice of two limes or lemons, add the rest of the spices and a tsp of salt and one of pepper. Hot sauce may be an option here also. Blend and make a green sauce. Pour over the cooked salmon and hopefully you already had one or two bottles of Sauvignon Blanc.

I served the salmon with garlic potatoes which I did by peeling a few potatoes; cubing them in about one inch sections and cooking them in a skillet with olive oil on medium low temp. Salt and pepper them well. Squeeze a world of garlic with a garlic press on those suckers, go crazy! It will keep all vampires away! , I also had homemade apple cobbler (which did not turned out well due to the doe being too moist I think I'm NOT a baker).

As the candles provided a warm glow, the armed forces radio from the nearby Navy base at Rota was playing great music and giving some sports updates. After diner we sipped on some Licor43 and drifted in thought, the winds had picked up outside and the temperature had dropped, the candle went out as we heard Silent Night on the radio.

Eve had to get back to England the 29th to spend New Years with her family. That day I drove her to the airport and said good bye once more. It seems like I'm always saying good bye to someone I care for.

Spring finally brought all the smells and flowers to Sevilla, orange blossoms permeated the air of festivities brought about by all the spring fairs and rituals. Bull fighting posters appeared all over the walls. We did all the usual things that had become common place for that month, the Holy Week processions , the Sevilla fair, the dancing and great consumptions of Fino Sherry. The school year plus the festivities had taken its toll. We decided to take a trip to the Huelva province south of Seville, to a town called Matalascanas. This was a beach town with a large number of German tourists and residents, a very unique town. It was always exciting to see the beach, however, this was nothing like back home, ice water, coarse sand, but hell, it was a beach. I had a very good friend who owned a restaurant there, an Italian who had married a woman from Spain and had settled in Matalascañas. By the way, the "n" in the name of the town is actually an "n" with a little worm on the top but like it's mentioned before in this book, Bill Gates Ah ain't and my "computereese" is faulty, so I just don't know how to add that little "worm" to the "n" which changes its pronounciation.

Pino's restaurant was Italian (of course) and was equipped with stone ovens that produced incredible tasting dishes (see, we're back to food) along with great open grills. Every time I visited Pino, I helped him in the kitchen and managed to pick up some pointers and make his day easier. The trip to Matalascañas takes about two hours, a beautiful old road with almost no traffic which is lined with Eucalyptus trees for most of the way. I drove with the top down and almost became overwhelmed with the smell from the trees. Pablo fell asleep within 20 minutes into the drive. After partying in Seville for 3 weeks we were both exhausted. I looked forward to relaxing and seeing Pino again.

Arriving late in the afternoon and after greeting Pino and his family with hugs he asked us the stupid question "are you guys hungry?" Dahh!!!!

28- PINO'S LAMB CHOPS

- One handful of minced parsley
- One cup of olive oil
- 1/2 cup of oregano
- 1/2 cup of lemon juice
- 4 cloves of minced garlic (surprised?)
- The ever present 5 oz. of dry sherry
- Salt and pepper
- And…yeah, lamb chops. Four or six medium chops

Rub the chops with olive oil, salt and pepper. Mix the rest of the ingredients well in a blender with more olive oil until you have the consistency of a Pesto sauce. Crown the chops on both sides on the grill on medium heat, bathe with the sauce (not you, the chops!) and grill for 20 minutes or so. Keep on basting them. I like lamb well done but some like to serve them medium. That's up to you. Medium means there is some pink in the middle. The thickness of the chops obviously plays a key role here.

We ate, drank some German beer from a tap and joked with Pino about opening a Pizzeria in Miami or New York while he broke a few dishes trying to show how well he could throw the pizza dough. His restaurant was close to the water and we could hear the waves gently pounding on the beach. We finished the night around 2 AM with the restaurant closed and drinking a bottle of Fino La Ina, another good sherry brand but not as good as Tio Pepe. Pino listened to all my latest romantic tales with interest, made several comments about the radio show which he could pick up and offered me a job singing at the restaurant. I told him he had a few too many Sherries. He finally gave me a final advice before hitting the sack which consisted in finding a good Italian girl, marrying her and having 10 kids! It was a great fun night, relaxing among friends, away from Seville, down by the ocean. Walking on the beach for the next few days brought some much needed sanity back to my brain. Pablo and I played Frisbee, something that at the time was foreign to Spain, this attracted a few German girls to play with us with little regard for the small bathing suite tops and the "bare" facts uncovered trying to catch my smart Frisbee.

The time to go back to Seville for final exams had arrived. Pino knew this was to be my last year in Spain and gave me a big hug as he told me I was "familia", his family, and if there was anything I ever needed, come to him. Somehow the theme from the movie "The Godfather" kept on ringing in my ear as Pablo and I packed our sun tanned bodies in the Fiat and headed back to Seville.

The trip back was an experiment in reality; soon another "rotation" would start in my life, (again, terms from Bro Peterson). Hospital rotations back in the states, responsibilities, and long working hours. I kept on telling myself that The Viking will still be The Viking. Final exams came and went just like that, almost anti-climactic.

My time in Spain was finished; it seemed like yesterday when I was walking on South Beach getting ready for the Spain rotation. You are probably wondering, especially female readers about all the "loose ends", the romantic stories. Well, yes, some tears were shed and no promises were made, that was impossible. It's not worth it going into details on all the good byes. It was not an easy thing to do. Those things never are. I did keep in touch with Asu, Eve, and Nuntxi for a while, wrote a few songs and kept them in my memory file. New places and events were ahead. A book could be written about the years at Memorial Hospital back in the states where my "Bro" Dr. Alan Peterson and I would enjoy some incredible times. I'm really not sure he wants me to write about those years...just kidding.

Not enough for the female curious reader? Ok, just to show I do have a sensitive side, one day I did receive a wedding invitation from Eve with a hand written note that said: I still love you, why? Why? I carried the note during my rotations at the hospital and often asked myself the same question. Asu also found someone as life goes on, her parents wrote me a very sweet letter and reminded me I would always be a son to them. I was happy for Asu; she deserved the stability I could not provide and all the good things life had to offer. A couple of years later I received a picture of new newborn baby boy. (NO, she didn't name him after me!). Nuntxi became a Psychologist and moved to Seville (Umm, wonder why...) There were many others I didn't mention in this book, had to have room for the recipes! I loved them all. Life has twists and turns. Sometimes the answer to your questions lies hidden in a drop of morning spring dew. Hope you catch that drop and taste it.

Good night my friends, I hope you enjoyed this book as much as I did. Many times while working late, I would envision you, the reader, trying out a recipe and wondering about the next girl or town. It is my hope that perhaps this book provided some fun and maybe helped you re-kindle some dreams in all of us.

Addendum
Forward to 2003

I thought it a good idea to travel forward in time and add sort of a bridge to the 21st century by introducing you to Rosas' Deli.

The best Cuban Food in the world is found in Cuba's seventh province, Miami. Since Castro's power grab more than 43 years ago, nearly two million people have escaped hell's island by any available means. A great number have lost their lives either through the hands of Cuba's state police or by drowning in the Florida straight trying to make the 90 mile trip in anything that floats. This tremendous influx of people has produced a large number of Cuban restaurants throughout the years in Miami (Dade County), Versailles restaurant, one of the oldest, has become a landmark. However, my favorite place in Broward County just north of Miami is called Rosa's Deli which is inside a gas station, you heard right, actually you didn't "hear", you "read" right. I have lunch at Rosa's almost every day. Oslayda cooks up a storm from a small kitchen the size of a compact car. Typical Cuban food is cooked to perfection. The smell of Cuban coffee permeates the air. Marta and Josie always serve the food with love and a smile. Rosa, (The Rosa's Deli Rosa), Hector and Homero always join in conversation and share a few jokes. By the way, you can also fill your tank with gas after eating Cuban roasted chicken, black beans, rice and Yuca con mojo.

Rosa's Deli is located in Ft. Lauderdale at the Chevron station on the corner of Cypress Creek Road and Lyons Road across from the old Cleveland Clinic building.

SPICES, SPICES, SPICES

GARLIC!!!!!!

Next to salt, garlic rules! It is the most commonly known food stuff in the world. Seen as both food and having medicinal properties, garlic's history goes back to pre-recorded time. We know the ancient Egyptians ate a large form of garlic. They ate so much of it that some historians claim that was the reason Moses took his people out of there. Egyptian garlic breath! (Just when you thought this book was going to get serious). It is also said that Roman soldiers used to rub garlic on their feet for quickness in battle and the Greeks used it as a symbol of courage and strength. Today we know garlic contains a substance called Kyolic which acts as a blood thinner and may be beneficial in certain heart conditions. Garlic was referred to in the old Soviet Union as Russian penicillin. The main reason to use garlic in my opinion is for the taste! Buy it fresh and don't store it in the refrigerator where it can dry and loose aroma. I like to buy the long braids of garlic and hang them in my kitchen. One of my fondest childhood memories is watching my father having breakfast which consisted of a bucket of "cafÈ con leche" (Cuban coffee and milk) and a hunk of Cuban bread dipped in olive oil and mashed garlic with a pinch of salt. My mouth just waters thinking about it. Special K???? Eat your heart out! My father died at 93 with cholesterol of 180.

Here is s tip to get the garlic smell out of your hands so you can enjoy the after meal romantic activity with your partner, just moisten your hands and rub with salt. I don't mind the smell of garlic though, I'm waiting for someone to come up with garlic toothpaste, garlic ice cream, garlic cologne etc. Finally, I have never seen a vampire in my kitchen so that last property of garlic may just be true.

CORIANDER

Also known as Cilantro is one of my favorite spices. Cilantro HAS to be fresh, the powder is tasteless. There are two types of Cilantro, one looks just like Italian Parsley and the other (a better one) looks like a long leaf 3 to 4 inches long with prickly edges. This type is harder to find but much more flavorful and aromatic. Try Cilantro on chicken soup. You can use it instead of basil on my basil tomato salad. On shrimp Creole is a must. You might not find fresh cilantro in Montana. There is a chance however where you find a Mexican community as Cilantro is used in salsa.

CUMIN

I love Cumin. Cumin is ok in the powder form and can be found almost anywhere. Cumin comes from the Curry family and goes great with Pork and Chicken.

BAY LEAVES

Great on roasts, a must when you do Delia's Boliche. Bay leaves maintain their flavor for a long time, years, when kept in a close jar.

PARSLEY

Fresh, fresh, fresh, lots of it. Don't use it for decoration or garnish, eat it!

OREGANO

Powder is ok, pork, chicken and of course Italian pasta sauce. Just don't overwhelm the food with it.

BASIL

Have you noticed the spices are not in alphabetical order and there must be a reason for this. I just don't know it. Purple Basil, Green Basil, you'll need some for the Basil tomatoes.

PEPPER

Fresh pepper is best. Invest in a good pepper mill, be cool. Try different varieties.

SAFFRON

Great spice usually found in Spanish markets. Saffron is made out of a flower and in its pure form it can be expensive. You can also find it in "hair" the Broadway musical, c'mon just playing with ya. In hair form that is. You will need Saffron for the Paella and the Arroz con Pollo recipes. Badia brand has it in this hair form packaged in small plastic boxes. Five hairs should be enough to give the rice a nice rich yellow color and that special taste. I usually throw the whole box in, live it up! Badia brand is usually found throughout South Florida.

VINEGAR

Balsamic should be what you use. It I a little more expensive but you don't need much. A decent bottle can be found for around $5.00 dollars unless you want to go to town and pay $20.00 for a fancy brand.

YOU ARE NOW ABOUT TO ENTER THE BEER ZONE, A DIMENSION NOT ONLY OF SIGHT BUT OF TASTE.

BEER

As with wines, your particular taste has a lot to do with your taste for beer. According to recent evidence, beer has been brewed as long as wine. There are so many brands of beer since the inception of mini-breweries that would be impossible to mention. One reason I wrote this page is to mention about a beer from my childhood, no you fool, I didn't drink beer as a kid, and it's just for memories sake. Growing up in PKC (Pre Kastro Cuba) there were many beers. Perhaps the most popular was one called "Hatuey".

Hatuey was the sponsor of the main evening news TV program where the main newscaster would sign off every night with the phrase: The news has been brought to you by Hatuey, the great beer of Cuba" and immediately this would follow with the "downing" in one shot, without coming up for air of a large stein filled with Hatuey. Imagine Brit Hume on FOX news doing the same thing with Budweiser! If you are ever in South Florida, order an Hatuey, no, they do not sponsor my book, but it is great beer.

Beer should not be consumed in a bottle unless there are no glasses. Sometimes it's a guy thing, I know. Beer should be consumed (like wine) in a proper glass, stein, tall glass, pint glass etc. The bottle changes the taste. Beer should always be fresh. The "born on date" campaign by Budweiser does make sense. If you have had that bottle of beer in the back of the refrigerator for more than 6 months, give it to the dog or pour it on a plant!

Finally, beer is also for the ladies. Listen you female readers; men (real men) love to see a woman drink a beer as this makes them feel more secure. They will feel you are one of the guys and be more sincere with you. You even get free relationship advice in this book. What a deal!

NOW LET'S GO INTO THE WINE ZONE

I decided to do a wine page in a generic way by grape!

As wine consumption in the United States has risen tremendously in the last twenty years, many restaurants have added extensive wine menus. This sometimes can be intimidating since prices can go from $15.00 dollars a bottle to $500.00 dollars or more. You might end up drinking beer (which is ok) or doing the "Yuppie" thing and ordering some fancy water bottle from France. If that's the case, at least order American water!

So, this simple guide might help you to choose a wine. Sometimes a taste for certain wines ahs to be developed. One must fine the common ground between what is proper etiquette and something you like. First rule I'm sure you know since it was illustrated in the James Bond film "From Russia With Love" when Bond started to suspect something was wrong with a spy from SPECTER passing as a British agent ordered white wine with filet of sole. So, Red wine with meats and white wine with fish, light reds like Merlot and Burgundy with chicken.

VARIETAL CHARACTERISTICS

In order to appreciate wine, it helps to understand the characteristics of different grapes. Same as trying to understand the characteristics of different women except grapes are simpler. (OK, ladies, just a little joke for the guys, I have picked on them as well). Cabernet Sauvignon, Merlot, Zinfandel all have different personalities. There may be some variations depending on the region, techniques etc. but certain qualities do remain. I will not go into different brands and wineries, you are really the bottom line here, as long as you like it and follow some simple etiquette you are fine.

CARBERNET SAUVIGNON

This is by far my favorite wine! (That's why it's listed first). It is considered the King of red wines. The region of Bordeaux in France has used this grape since the 18th century, always mixing it with Cabernet Franc and Merlot. This grape however is found everywhere in the world including the Napa Valley in California which has superb Cabernet Sauvignon.

Cabernet's flavors have been described as currant, plum, black cherry, spice, mint, cedar, anise, olive, oregano and many more. The higher the percentage of Cabernet grape, the more complex the flavor becomes. I like to describe my Cabernet as woody without a bite and dry but with body and character. Cabernets start out dark purple, ruby in color with firm acidity, a firm body and great intensity. Notice that women can be described the same way. So many similarities!

I like Cabernets from Napa, California. There is a Cabernet-Shiraz blend from Australia called St. Jacob's Creek which is excellent and not expensive at all (about 8 to 10 dollars a bottle). Cabernets go great with steak; the flavor of a T-bone on the grill followed by a sip of Cabernet can only be described as uplifting to the soul. I must tell you, do NOT put ice in any of these wines or I'll find out through my publisher where you live and I'll come to your house and confiscate the book! No refunds!

MERLOT

Next to Cabernet, Merlot is probably my next favorite wine (that's why is listed second). Merlot has been a very popular wine through the nineties. It's sometimes used for a blend in Bordeaux but it can stand alone as well. Merlots are lighter than Cabernets and fit very well with stews, chicken, lamb. It's difficult to grow Merlot grapes in California since it tends to ripen unevenly. Many experts agree that Washington State had a very good Merlot crop in the year 2000.

Other reds that need to be mentioned are the Rioja's from Spain. They go not only with meats but provide wonderful company to Paella and Arroz con Pollo. Some brands to look for, Paternina blue ribbon, Marques del Riscal, and one of the very best, Faustino gran reserva. You can not go wrong with these wines.

So much for reds. Notice I did not include Chianti's from Italy in the mix. For my taste, Chianti's have to be very good to enjoy and besides, Chianti's remind me of my college days when they came in those long neck bottles decorated in wicker material with a string to hanging from it. I do like other Italian wines like Brillante and from the Umbria region. I am just not crazy about Chianti; however I do like Italian cheeses and Italian women.

PINOT NOIR

This is really great red wine. There is a very special Pinot Noir called Domaine Druhin from Oregon State. This wine will fill your dreams with beauty (that's a new way to describe a wine!). Because of its soil quality, Oregon State grows the best Pinot Noir grapes in the world. Pinot Noir is a very delicate fickle grape that reacts strongly to environmental changes such as heat and cold spells. This wine goes great with Chicken Marsala, pastas etc.

Ok, I guess I have to mention white wines. First, forget the sweet stuff, that's for wimps or dessert. In a rare cosmic event I may drink a white wine, very dry and very chilled but NO ice in the wine ok?

SAUVIGNON BLANC

This wine has a noticeable aroma often described as "musky". The pure variety is found in Loire and Pouilli-Fume as part of a blend. It goes well with fish, salmon or shell fish. The Mendozas from Argentina are a good buy. A better buy is "Gato Negro" from Chile (about $ 10.00 dollars).

CHARDONNAY

This is considered the "King" of white wines. It makes very consistently rich and complex wines. California's Santa Barbara and Santa Maria Valley will make you happy ($ 12.00 to $ 16.00 dollars a bottle). Its flavor has been described as apple, figs, melon, lemon and other flavors.

Chablis, Semillon, and Fume Blanc are other white varieties you might enjoy. Some of you may be wondering about German wines, stay wondering. I love German beer, they make great cars also. Lastly I need to mention the Sherries from Jerez. I often visited the town called Jerez de la Frontera near Seville, Spain. The whole town is a winery; really, there are no houses there, only the finest Sherry wineries in the world. Try a chilled Tio Pepe before dinner, use the right glass. La Ina, Gonzales Byas are great as well. . Of course if you were already "well learned" as we say down south in the art of grape fermentation (wine making for those in Buffalo), you didn't have to read this section.

I will close this section with a profound statement about wine:

"Wine is good"

A LITTLE MORE SPICE

Adobo is often mentioned in this book and I am well aware this spice may not be available in far out places like Iowa or Kansas. Badia brand is my favorite. They are based in South Florida. I will provide their address if you wish to write them and perhaps they will send you a bottle along with information on all their products. An alternative is to make your own. It won't be quite the same, but here we go:

Mix

1/2 cup of garlic powder

1/2 cup of cumin powder

1/4 cup of salt

One teaspoon of pepper

1/2 cup of onion powder

A pinch of oregano

A wet version called Mojo:

1/2 cup of vinegar

1/2 cup of lime juice

1/2 cup of olive oil

One teaspoon of salt and one of pepper

5 fresh garlic cloves squeezed with a garlic press

1/4 cup of orange juice.

Use on pork, chicken as a marinade and for basting

About the Author

True to his "tropical guy" image, Fred Valdes lives in South Florida; he DID complete medical school (finally) and worked at a major hospital through the 90's. He is currently working on another book, playing his D-35 Martin guitar, writing more songs. Dr. Valdes hosted a radio show last year and has served as medical dept. chairman for City College, Ft. Lauderdale for the last 6 years. Dr. Valdes traded the Fiat Spider mentioned in the book for a large conversion van in order to better accommodate his lovely wife Janet (yep, he did finally get married) and his two beautiful daughters Vanessa and Monique.

Printed in the United States
16355LVS00003B/189-190

9 781594 081934